# Consumer Rights for Immigrants

*Other National Consumer Law Center Publications*

## Books for Consumers and Their Counselors

Surviving Debt: A Guide for Consumers
Return to Sender, Getting a Refund or Replacement for Your Lemon Car
How to Buy a Manufactured Home

## Legal Practice Manuals (all with CD-Roms)

*Debtor Rights Library:*
Consumer Bankruptcy Law and Practice
Fair Debt Collection
Repossessions and Foreclosures
Student Loan Law
Access to Utility Service

*Credit and Banking Library:*
Truth in Lending
Cost of Credit
Fair Credit Reporting Act
Credit Discrimination
Consumer Banking and Payments Law

*Consumer Litigation Library:*
Consumer Arbitration Agreements
Consumer Class Actions
Consumer Law Pleadings

*Deception and Warranties Library*
Unfair and Deceptive Acts and Practices
Consumer Warranty Law
Automobile Fraud

## Other Publications for Lawyers

NCLC REPORTS newsletter
Consumer Law in a Box CD-Rom
Stop Predatory Lending

# The National Consumer Law Center Guide to

# Consumer Rights for Immigrants

From
THE NATIONAL CONSUMER LAW CENTER,
America's Consumer Law Experts

*Principal Authors*

Deanne Loonin

Chi Chi Wu

For reprint permissions or ordering information, contact Publications, NCLC, 77 Summer Street, 10th Floor, Boston, MA 02110-1006, (617) 523-8010, Fax (617) 523-7398, E-mail: consumerlaw@nclc.org

ISBN 1-931697-14-0

This project was supported by the Open Society Institute

10 9 8 7 6 5 4 3 2 1

This book is intended to provide accurate and authoritative information in regard to the subject matter covered. This book cannot substitute for the independent judgment and skills of a competent attorney or other professional. Non-attorneys are cautioned against using these materials in conducting litigation without advice or assistance from an attorney or other professional. Non-attorneys are also cautioned against engaging in conduct which might be considered the unauthorized practice of law.

Cover design and illustration by Lightbourne Images, copyright © 2002.

# ABOUT THE AUTHORS

**Deanne Loonin** is a staff attorney at National Consumer Law Center, focusing on consumer issues affecting low-income seniors and immigrants, as well as student loan and credit discrimination issues. She is co-director of NCLC's Immigrant Consumer Rights Initiative. Ms. Loonin previously worked as a staff attorney at Bet Tzedek Legal Services in Los Angeles, directing Bet Tzedek's senior consumer fraud unit.

**Chi Chi Wu** is a staff attorney at National Consumer Law Center, focusing on consumer issues affecting immigrants, domestic violence victims, and low-income seniors, as well as electronic benefits transfer, fair credit reporting, and credit discrimination issues. She is co-director of NCLC's Immigrant Consumer Rights Initiative. Ms. Wu was formerly an Assistant Attorney General with the Consumer Protection Division of the Massachusetts Attorney General's Office, where she focused on consumer fraud cases involving immigrant victims.

# ACKNOWLEDGMENTS

This handbook was made possible through a grant from the Open Society Institute. Special thanks also to the Joyce Mertz Gilmore Foundation for their initial support of this project.

Many members of the NCLC staff made significant contributions to this handbook. In particular, the authors thank Jon Sheldon, Donna Wong, Denise Lisio, and Mica Astion for production assistance.

# ABOUT NCLC

The National Consumer Law Center, a nonprofit corporation founded in 1969 and dedicated to the interests of low-income consumers, provides consumer law and technical support and consulting services to legal services attorneys, government agencies, and private attorneys representing consumers.

In 1998, NCLC began a national initiative focusing on immigrant consumers. With the support of the Open Society Institute, this initiative was expanded into the Immigrant Justice in the Consumer Marketplace project. See our website for more information at www.consumerlaw.org/osi/index.htm.

NCLC conducts national, regional, and local consumer law trainings, including trainings focused on immigrant consumer issues. It also holds annual conferences on consumer rights litigation and other issues. Contact NCLC for more information.

## CASE CONSULTING

Case analysis and consulting for lawyers representing low-income consumers are among NCLC's primary activities. As part of the Immigrant Justice in the Consumer Marketplace Initiative, NCLC will provide free consultations to advocates representing immigrant consumers on many types of cases. Free consultations are available as long as resources permit. Additional free consultation may be available depending on funding.

## ORDERING PUBLICATIONS

Publications Department, National Consumer Law Center, 77 Summer St., 10<sup>th</sup> Fl., Boston, MA 02110-1006, (617) 523-8089; FAX (617) 523-7398; Email: publications@nclc.org.

## CHARITABLE DONATIONS

NCLC's work depends in part on the support of private donors. Tax deductible donations should be made payable to National Consumer Law Center, Inc. NCLC has also received generous court-approved *cy pres* awards arising from consumer class actions to advance the interests of class members.

# CONTENTS

## Appendices

# MARKETPLACE JUSTICE FOR NEW IMMIGRANTS

Having made the often difficult journey to the United States in search of opportunity, America's newest residents all too often find themselves easy prey to the consumer abuses that thrive in the low-income communities in which many of them live. They must learn to access telephone and utility services, to protect themselves from landlord exploitation, to buy and insure a car, to avoid unscrupulous high-rate lenders, and to negotiate successfully all the other consumer choices which daily impact their lives. These marketplace decisions have as big an impact on their economic health as does the size of their paychecks.

Credit and banking issues, in particular, negatively affect immigrants making consumer choices as they adjust to American life, enter the work force, seek education, and open bank accounts. A wave of deregulatory fervor in the last two decades has removed many of the mechanisms that once curbed marketplace abuses. Check cashers, finance companies, rent-to-own, and other sub-prime lenders, now virtually unregulated, prey upon low-income and immigrant communities.[1]

Additional consumer abuses stem from and play upon immigrant fears about the fragility of their legal status. Immigration consultants and *notarios* take advantage of an individual's desperation, inability to speak or read English, and unfamiliarity with the legal system. Some falsely claim that they can expedite naturalization; many specialize in housing, bankruptcy, and other credit concerns that could result in victims losing their homes and/ or forfeiting important rights. The consequences of these scams and the failure of many consultants to provide even minimally competent legal advice are devastating for immigrants trying to build productive lives in a new country.

Unfortunately, limited fluency in English and unfamiliarity with the American marketplace make immigrants particularly vulnerable to consumer abuses. Also troubling is the fact that they suffer disproportionately when they fall victim to marketplace abuses because they are less likely to seek help for legal problems than are other low-income consumers. Cultural and psychological barriers explain part of this hesitancy: many immigrants are distrustful of the legal system, for example, having come from countries with more arbitrary and prejudicial systems of justice.

In 1998, the National Consumer Law Center (NCLC) began a national Immigrant Consumer Rights Initiative to help address the legal needs of low-income immigrants experiencing financial problems that hinder economic independence. The Emma Lazarus Fund and the Joyce-Mertz Gilmore Foundation initially supported this work. In 2001, thanks to generous support from the Open Society Institute, NCLC began expanding this project.

A primary goal of the project is to link the legal community, particularly legal services and pro bono resources, with advocates who work closely with immigrants and refugees. Although there are challenges ahead, the unique barriers to justice in immigrant communities should not mask the unique strengths. Many immigrants and refugees bring to this country thriving networks of cooperation to support them as they learn to adapt to the society, culture, and economy of the United States.

NCLC will be working with state and local immigrant advocates, helping to develop bridges between these groups and pro bono and legal services attorneys. In 2001, we concentrated our efforts in two cities, Philadelphia and Chicago. In 2002, we plan to expand the project nationally, encouraging and supporting other immigrant advocates and attorneys across the country in establishing similar programs.

This handbook provides an introduction for advocates to many of the most critical consumer issues faced by low-income immigrants. More extensive resources are cited throughout. In addition to providing an introduction to key consumer problems and remedies, this handbook contains some straightforward consumer information that can be used in assisting clients.

Updated information about the project can be found at www.nclc.org/osi/index.htm.

---

[1] The term "immigrant" used throughout this handbook refers to newcomers to the United States. The category includes citizens and noncitizens, English speakers and non-English speakers, refugees and non-refugees. Most of these clients can still be assisted by programs funded by the Legal Services Corporation (LSC) despite the recent cuts and restrictions. More information on the LSC restrictions is available from the Center for Law & Social Policy, (202) 328-5140, http://www.clasp.org. The National Immigration Law Center also has information on the LSC restrictions. (213) 639-3900, http://www.nilc.org.

# -- 2 --

# CONSUMER LAW RESOURCES

- *Resources from National Consumer Law Center*
- *Selected Resources on Consumer and Immigrant Issues*
- *Helpful Websites*

## THE NATIONAL CONSUMER LAW CENTER (NCLC)

The National Consumer Law Center publishes the consumer credit and sales legal practice series, including manuals on consumer remedies for credit, sales, and collection practices. For more information, contact NCLC publications at 617-523-8089, or visit NCLC's website, www.consumerlaw.org.

National Consumer Law Center
77 Summer St., 10th Floor
Boston, MA 02110-1006
(617) 523-8010

Also available from NCLC:

*Surviving Debt: A Guide for Consumers* (3d ed. 1999).

NCLC REPORTS newsletters: Bankruptcy and Foreclosures edition, Debt Collection and Repossessions edition, Consumer Credit and Usury edition, and Deceptive Practices and Warranties edition.

A current order form for NCLC pamphlets and brochures is printed at the back of this Handbook. (Appendix 3)

## SELECTED RESOURCES ON CONSUMER AND IMMIGRANT ISSUES

Laurence Canter and Martha Siegel, *U.S. Immigration Made Easy*, Nolo Press (8th ed. 2001). Available from Nolo Press, 1-800-992-6656 or www.nolo.com.

Catholic Legal Immigration Network, Inc. (CLINIC) and National Immigration Law Center, *Affidavit of Support and Sponsorship Requirements: A Practitioner's Guide* (1998). To order, contact CLINIC, 415 Michigan Ave., NE, Washington, D.C. 20017.

Deanna Kitamura and Deanne Loonin, "Getting Credit Where Credit Is Due: Helping Welfare-to-Work Clients Address Credit-Reporting Issues," 34 Clearinghouse Review 148 (July/August 2000).

Deanne Loonin, Kathleen Michon and David Kinnecome, "Fraudulent *Notarios*, Document Preparers, and Other Nonattorney Service Providers: Legal Remedies for a Growing Problem," 31 Clearinghouse Review 327 (Nov./Dec. 1997).

Deanne Loonin and Elizabeth Renuart, "Less Than Six Degrees of Separation: Consumer Law Connections to Your Practice," Parts I and II, 31 Clearinghouse Review 584 (March/April 1998), 32 Clearinghouse Review 3 (May/June 1998).

Joanne I. Moore, ed., *Immigrants in Courts* (University of Washington Press 1999).

National Immigration Law Center, *Update* (newsletter). To order, contact NILC, 3435 Wilshire Blvd., Suite 2850, Los Angeles, CA 90010. (213) 639-3900.

Elizabeth Renuart and Jean Ann Fox, "Payday Loans: A High Cost for a Small Loan in Low Income and Working Communities," 35 Clearinghouse Review 589 (Jan/Feb. 2001).

Odette Williamson, "Protecting Elder Homeowners From Predatory Mortgage Lenders," 34 Clearinghouse Review 297 (Sept./Oct. 2000).

# HELPFUL WEB SITES

## Immigrant and Immigrant Rights-Related Sites

American Bar Association (ABA) Immigration Pro Bono
Development Project
www.abanet.org/immigprobono/home.html
740 15th St., NW
Washington, D.C. 20005-1022
202-662-1698

American Civil Liberties Union (ACLU)
www.aclu.org
125 Broad St., 18th Fl.
New York, NY 10004
212-344-3005

American Immigration Lawyers Association (AILA)
www.aila.org
1400 Eye St., NW
Suite 1200
Washington, D.C. 20005
202-216-2400

Catholic Legal Immigration Network (CLINIC)
www.cliniclegal.org
415 Michigan Ave., NE
Washington, D.C. 20017
202-635-2556
Immigrant Legal Resource Center (ILRC)
www.ilrc.org
1663 Mission St., Suite 602

San Francisco, CA  94102
415-255-1056

National Immigration Forum
www.immigrationforum.org
220 I Street, NE #220
Washington, D.C.  20002
202-544-0004

National Immigration Law Center
www.nilc.org
3435 Wilshire Blvd.
Suite 2850
Los Angeles, CA  90010
213-639-3900

## Credit Bureaus (and to order credit reports)

Equifax: www.equifax.com

Experian (formerly TRW): www.experian.com

Transunion: www.tuc.com

## General Consumer And Legal Sites

American Bankruptcy Institute
www.abiworld.org

Better Business Bureau
www.bbb.org

Center on Budget and Policy Priorities
www.cbpp.org

Consumers Union
www.consumersunion.org
National Association of Consumer Advocates
www.naca.net

National Consumer Law Center
www.consumerlaw.org

Poverty Law Center
www.povertylaw.org

Urban Institute
www.urban org

## Selected Government Sites

Department of Education
www.ed.gov
For information on student financial assistance.

Federal Trade Commission (FTC)
www.ftc.gov/bcp/menu-credit.htm
To view FTC publications on consumer credit rights.

Immigration and Naturalization Service (INS)
www.ins.doj.gov

Internal Revenue Service
www.irs.ustreas.gov
An IRS site that is helpful in answering basic tax filing and other questions.

Government Services Agency
www.pueblo.gsa.gov
The government's consumer information center. Contains direct links to federal indexes and agencies, consumer-help organizations, community nets and other sites providing helpful consumer information.

# BUDGETING AND PRIORITIZING DEBT

- *Setting Up a Budget*
- *Maximizing Income*
- *Minimizing Expenses*
- *Protecting the Family Income and Assets from Attachment by Creditors*
- *Prioritizing Debt*

The ultimate goal in working with low-income immigrants and with all low-income clients is to help the clients get out of poverty. At the most basic level this means helping people maximize their incomes and reduce their expenses. Just as welfare advocates specialize in getting clients as much income as possible from public assistance and other sources, consumer law advocates focus on minimizing clients' expenses through effective budgeting, avoiding predatory lenders and other high cost credit sources, and avoiding consumer scams that bleed low-income clients' limited resources.

## SETTING UP A BUDGET

If an immigrant is having financial trouble, it is essential that she sets up (and tries to stay on) and income and expense budget. The budget will help the immigrant:

- Determine how much money she has to cover necessities and how much is left to pay bills. This will help establish the range of options the immigrant has to deal with her bills.

- Guide spending habits. The budget is based on the best planning about what the immigrant needs. If she can live within the budget, she can be assured that she is not overspending and making problems worse.

- If the immigrant is having trouble meeting all her bills, she may want to work with creditors that offer options for a payment plan or modification of debt. The immigrant's ability to qualify for these programs will be based on her budget. If the immigrant has already done some the work to develop a budget, she will have a sense of what she can afford to offer creditors. She will also be able to provide basic information to creditors, which will make the process move more smoothly and give her additional credibility.

A sample budget form is included at the end of this Handbook in Appendix 1.

## MAXIMIZING INCOME

While many advocates are adept at helping clients apply for various federal and state government benefits, there are a couple of programs often overlooked and worth mentioning:

- **Earned Income Tax Credit.** The Earned Income Tax Credit is a frequently overlooked means of increasing a client's income if she is employed. Even if the client has not qualified for this credit in the past, a change in income or a lay-off may make the client eligible during a year in which she has financial problems. The amount of the tax credit is based on the amount of income and family size. If the client is employed and the total income falls below a threshold amount, she qualifies for the credit even if the client does not owe the government any money.

Immigrants are more apt than most low-income consumers to overlook the Earned Income Tax Credit. A recent study by the Urban Institute found that Hispanic immigrants are less likely to know about the tax credit than non-Hispanics.[1] The Center for Budget & Policy Priorities is a good resource for information on the Earned Income Tax Credit (www.cbpp.org), and has educational materials available in a variety of languages.

- **Utility Assistance Programs.** These days, utility bills are often one of the steepest expenses faced by our clients. There are a number of energy assistance programs, including the federal Low Income Home Energy Assistance Program (LIHEAP), that can help. More information on these programs is included in Chapter 12, Telephone and Utility Issues.

As most immigrant advocates know, immigrant eligibility for public assistance programs is a complex issue. For information on this issue, the National Immigration Law Center publishes a *Guide to Immigrant Eligibility for Federal Programs* (4th ed. 2001), which you can order from www.nilc.org/pubs/orderfrm.htm. Advocates for non-citizen immigrants should also consult NILC's community education materials on the public charge issue, available at www.nilc.org/ce/ceindex.htm.

## MINIMIZING EXPENSES

An important means of lowering family expenses is to reduce or eliminate the debts that the family owes. Consumer law can be extremely helpful in reaching this goal. Examples of where consumer law can reduce or eliminate debt are:

- Defenses against mortgage foreclosure and car repossession.

- Defenses against unconscionably priced loans and goods.

- Protections from overreaching creditors and collectors, including abusive debt collectors.

- Access to reasonably priced energy and credit.

- Discharges of student loans or reduction of monthly payments.

- Bankruptcy.

This handbook includes chapters that cover many of the above issues. These issues are also addressed more extensively in *Surviving Debt*, written for consumers and published by the National Consumer Law Center. This publication can be ordered by calling the NCLC Publications Department at (617) 523-8089.

## PROTECTING THE FAMILY INCOME AND ASSETS FROM ATTACHMENTS BY CREDITORS

Another part of the budget equation involves knowledge about how to protect a family's income and assets from judgment creditors. Advocates should be familiar with various federal and state laws that protect debtors such as:

- **Protections for wage garnishment.**
  Federal law protects the first $154.50 of weekly take-home pay from garnishment. If weekly take-home pay exceeds $154.50, the judgment creditor still cannot take more than 25% of take-home pay. (This protection does not apply to garnishment for child support or alimony.) Several states provide even greater protections.

- **Protections against attachment of public benefits.**
  Most public assistance benefits are exempt from attachment under state law. Supplemental Security Income (SSI) and Social Security payments are exempt under federal law. Veteran's benefits are exempt under the Veteran's Administration Act. However, these benefits can sometimes

be attached by government agencies trying to collect money owed to them.

- **Protections against attachment of pension and retirement benefits.**
  Federal law and most states exempt from attachment at least a portion of benefits received under various employee retirement or pension plans.

- **Protections for real and personal property in the hands of the family or held by others (e.g., bank accounts).**
  Every state protects at least some minimum amount of personal and real property from attachment, though the amounts vary greatly from state to state. Some states have special protections for the family home.

When all of the income and assets of the client are protected by state and federal exemption and garnishment laws, creditors can do nothing to collect from the client until and unless the family income and assets increase. This is called being "judgment-proof." That is to say, though the creditors may sue on a debt and obtain a court judgment in the amount owed, there may be no way that the creditor can effectively collect this debt from the consumer. Helping clients understand this fact can alleviate a great deal of family stress.

## PRIORITIZING DEBT

Low-income consumers frequently have trouble keeping all of their debts up to date. This is not surprising since family income is so limited that it cannot always stretch far enough to pay all of the household expenses each month. This leaves some families with no choice but to delay or not pay some debts.

Once the client determines that not all of the household bills can be paid as they come due, the client will have to make hard choices about which bills to pay first. The home or apartment, utility service, the car, and even household possessions may be at stake. Following the rules described below may make the difference between keeping or losing important property.

The most important principle in setting priorities is understanding the concept of "collateral." Collateral is property which a creditor has the right to seize if the client does not pay a particular debt. The most common forms of collateral are the family home in the case of a mortgage (or deed of trust) and the car in the case of most car loans. A creditor may also have collateral in household goods, business property, bank account, or even wages. When a creditor has taken collateral for the loan, it has a "lien" on the property.

Creditors who have collateral are usually referred to as "secured" creditors. They have the security of knowing that they can take the collateral and sell it to get their money. Creditors without collateral are often referred to as "unsecured." It is usually hard for unsecured creditors to collect what they are owed unless the consumer pays voluntarily.

Consumers must determine which of their debts are "secured" and which are "unsecured." They should almost always pay secured debts first. Instead of delaying or eliminating certain debt repayments, clients may be tempted to take on more debt to repay old debts. This is generally a bad idea. The best strategy in dealing with too much debt is deciding which debts to pay first, which debts the client can refuse to pay, and which debts can be put off until later. The most important creditor to pay is not necessarily the creditor that screams the loudest or the most often. Creditors who yell the loudest often do so only because they have no better way to get their money than to intimidate the client into paying. Of more concern are creditors who not only threaten, but actually can take quick action against the residence, utility service, car, or other important assets.

Clients should direct their limited resources to what is most necessary for the family--typically food, clothing, shelter and utility service. Unfortunately, there is no magic list of the order in which debts should be paid. Everyone's situation will be different. Instead, what follows are sixteen rules about how to set priorities.

- **Always Pay Family Necessities First.**
  Usually this means food and unavoidable medical expenses.

- **Next Pay Housing-Related Bills.**

Families must keep up the mortgage or rent payments if at all possible. If the client owns the home, real estate taxes and insurance must also be paid unless they are included in the monthly mortgage payment. Similarly, any condo fees or mobile home lot payments should be considered a high priority. Failure to pay these debts can lead to loss of the home.

- **Pay the Minimum Required to Keep Essential Utility Service.**
  While this may not always require full and immediate payment of the entire amount of the bill, the minimum payment necessary to avoid disconnection should be made if at all possible. Working hard to keep the house or apartment makes little sense if the client cannot live there because there are no utilities.

- **Pay Car Loans or Leases Next if the Car Is Essential.**
  If the client needs the car to get to work or for other essential transportation, the car payment must be the next priority after food, housing costs, unavoidable medical expenses, and utilities. The client may even want to pay for the car first if the car is necessary to keep his/her job. The car insurance must be paid as well. Otherwise, the creditor may buy costly insurance at the client's expense. And in most states, it is illegal not to have automobile liability coverage.

- **The Client Must Pay Child Support Debts.**
  These debts will not go away and can result in very serious problems, including prison, for nonpayment.

- **Income Tax Debts Are Also High Priority.**
  Clients must pay any income taxes owed that are not automatically deducted from wages, and must file federal income tax returns even if they cannot afford to pay any balance due. The government has many collection rights which

other creditors do not have, particularly if the client does not file a return.

- **Loans Without Collateral Are Low Priority.**
  Most credit card debts, attorney, doctor and hospital bills, and other debts to professionals, open accounts with merchants, and similar debts are low priority. Clients have not pledged any collateral for these loans, and there is rarely anything that these creditors can do to hurt them in the short term. Many won't bother to try to collect in the long term.

- **Loans With Only Household Goods as Collateral Are Also Low Priority.**
  Sometimes a creditor requires the client to place some of the household goods as collateral on a loan. This loan can generally be treated the same as an unsecured debt -- as a low priority. Creditors rarely seize household goods because they have little market value, it is hard to seize them without involving the courts, and it is time consuming and expensive to use the courts to seize them.

- **Do <u>Not</u> Move a Debt Up in Priority Because the Creditor Threatens Suit.**
  Many threats to sue are not carried out. Even if the creditor does sue, it will take a while for the collector to be able to seize any property, and much of the family's property may be exempt from seizure. On the other hand, non-payment of rent, mortgage and car debts may result in immediate loss of the home or car.

- **Do Not Pay When There Are Good Legal Defenses to Repayment.**
  Some examples of legal defenses are that goods purchased were defective, or that the creditor is asking for more money than it is entitled to. If there is a legal defense, the client should obtain legal advice to determine whether the defense will succeed. In evaluating these options, remember that it is especially dangerous to withhold mortgage or rent payments without legal advice.

- **Court Judgments Move Up in Priority, But Often Less Than One Would Think.**
  After a collector obtains a court judgment, that debt often should move up in priority, because the creditor can enforce that judgment by asking the court to seize certain property, wages, and bank accounts. Nevertheless, how serious a threat this really is will depend on the state's law, the value of the property, and the amount of income. As discussed above, it may be that all of the client's property and wages are protected under state law. So, the client should pay off more pressing obligations first and then come back and pay this debt.

- **Student Loans Are Medium Priority Debts.**
  They should generally be paid ahead of low priority debts, but after top priority debts. Most delinquent student loans are backed by the United States. The law provides special collection remedies to the government which are not available to other creditors. These include seizure of tax refunds, special wage garnishment rules, and denial of new student loans and grants.

- **Debt Collection Efforts Should *Never* Move Up a Debt's Priority.**
  Clients should be polite to the collector, but make *their* own choices about which debts to pay based on what is best for the family. Debt collectors are unlikely to give good advice. Clients can easily stop debt collection contacts and they have legal remedies to deal with collection harassment.

- **Threats to Ruin One's Credit Record Should *Never* Move Up a Debt's Priority.**
  In many cases, when a collector threatens to report a delinquency to the credit bureau, the creditor has already provided the credit bureau with the exact status of the account. And if the creditor has not done so, a collector hired by the creditor is very unlikely to do so.

- ### Cosigned Debts Should Be Treated Like One's Other Debts.

  If the client has put up the home or car as collateral on a loan, that is a high priority debt if the other co-signers are not keeping the debt current. If the client has not put up such collateral, cosigned debts should be treated as a lower priority. If others have cosigned for the client and she is unable to pay the debt, the client should tell the cosigner about the financial problems so that the cosigner can decide what to do about that debt.

- ### Refinancing Is Rarely the Answer.

  Clients should always be careful about refinancing. It can be very expensive and it can give creditors more opportunities to seize important assets. A short term fix can lead to long term problems.

More detailed information on these topics can be found in *Surviving Debt* published by the National Consumer Law Center.

---

[1] Katherine Ross Phillips, "Who Know about the Earned Income Tax Credit?" The Urban Institute (January 2001).

# -- 4 --

# HIGH COST CREDIT

- *The High Cost of Different Kinds of Small Loans*
- *Alternative Sources of Credit*

The high cost of cashing checks, paying bills, renting household goods, and getting small loans in times of need bleed millions of dollars from the pockets of those least able to afford it.

Challenging high cost loans requires a multi-faceted approach including:

- **Education**. Clients need to know about the cost of credit and how much it impacts their budgets. When they understand the overall costs of using such lenders, clients will also want to know if there are alternatives, which will reduce their monthly expenses.

- **Alternative Sources of Credit.** Using low-cost checking and savings accounts (to the extent they are available in low-income neighborhoods) to avoid the costs of check cashers is a start. Credit unions make small loans to their members, which could be used to purchase appliances or pay medical and car repair bills. In addition, there are non-profits in every state that may make small business loans for those clients who wish to avoid high cost lenders when starting up their own businesses.

- **Legal Challenges**. Individual and class-wide litigation is another critical strategy. A number of NCLC publications are available to assist advocates with legal challenges against over-reaching creditors and lenders, including: NCLC's manuals, *The Cost of Credit: Regulation and Legal Challenges* (2d ed. 2000 and Supp.), and *Truth in Lending* (4th ed. 1999 and Supp.). A separate handbook on predatory lending issues is also available. NCLC also publishes a consumer education brochure, "Borrower Beware" that summarizes high cost lending issues (available in English, Spanish, Chinese, Korean, Vietnamese and Russian – see the order form in the back of this Handbook to order). For updates, see NCLC's web site, http://www.consumerlaw.org.

- **Legislation.** Advocates should focus on strengthening existing state, federal, and local laws, fighting industry-backed proposals, and developing new protections.

## THE HIGH COST OF DIFFERENT KINDS OF SMALL LOANS

**Payday Loans.** Payday loans go by a variety of names, including "deferred presentment," "cash advances," "deferred deposits," or "check loans," but they all work similarly. The consumer writes a check to the lender for the amount borrowed plus a fee that is either a percentage or a flat dollar amount, or signs an agreement to debit his or her bank account automatically. The typical annual percentage rate (APR) is at least 390% and averages close to 500%, though advocates and credit code enforcement agencies have noted rates of 1,300% to 7,300%. The check (or debit agreement) is then held for up to a month, usually until the customer's next payday or receipt of a government check. At that point, the consumer redeems the check by paying the face amount, allows the check to be cashed, or pays another fee to extend the loan.

These loans are marketed as a quick and easy way to get cash until the next payday. To qualify, consumers need only be employed for a period of time with the current employer or receive government benefits, maintain a personal checking account, and show a pay stub and bank statement. Credit reports are not routinely reviewed.

Immigrants without bank accounts or public benefits are for the most part unable to use these services. Advocates should be aware that efforts to encourage immigrants to open bank accounts (discussed in the next chapter) may have the unintended consequence of increasing payday lending use in these communities. This does not mean that new immigrants should avoid opening bank accounts. Instead, advocates need to educate new immigrants on the exorbitant expenses associated with payday lending and help develop less expensive alternatives.

Abuses in making and collecting payday loans occur in a variety of ways. Cash-strapped consumers are rarely able to repay the entire loan when payday arrives, because they need the new paycheck for current living expenses. Lenders encourage these consumers to rollover or refinance one payday loan with another. Those who do so pay yet another round of charges and fees and obtain no additional cash in return. If the check is returned for insufficient funds or the loan otherwise goes unpaid, the lender may threaten to involve the criminal justice system, a tactic that is possible only because a check, rather than a mere promissory note, is involved.

There are many legal claims available to challenge these loans. These are discussed in detail in NCLC's manual, *The Cost of Credit: Regulation and Legal Challenges* and in other NCLC publications.

**Pawnbrokers.** Pawnbrokers are companies that allow consumers to trade something of value such as jewelry or a stereo in exchange for cash. Usually, a pawnbroker will lend only one-half of the value of the property. The borrower must then pay back the loan within a certain period of time or the pawnbroker can sell the property and keep the money. Since borrowers are charged fees and only receive at most half the value of the property in cash, they may be paying up to 200% interest per year.

Almost every state has enacted laws that regulate pawnbrokers in some way. Most states set ceilings on interest rates and other fees that pawnshops can charge on loans.[1]

**Auto Title Pawns.** Auto title pawn transactions are a relatively new phenomena where the car owner pawns title to the car in exchange for a sum of cash. The lender may then claim title to the car and lease it back to the consumer. Others just hold onto the certificate of title without any attempt to transfer ownership. If the customer fails to pay the cash advanced plus interest and fees when due, the pawnbroker may attempt to repossess the car. The effective interest rate of an auto pawn can be astronomical, with annual percentage rates of over 900%.

For example:

---

- A consumer gives her car title ($1,000 value) and gets back half the value of the car = $500
- The consumer is required to pay weekly installments of $103.30 for 10 weeks
  ($103.30 x 10 weeks) = $1,033

  $1,033 paid
  - $ 500 received =
  _____
  $533   (828% interest on an annual basis)

---

There are several legal theories to attack auto title pawn practices, including the argument that the auto title pawnbroker is not a true pawnbroker because it does not retain possession of the pledged car. More information can be found in NCLC's manuals *The Cost of Credit: Regulation and Legal Challenges, Repossession and Foreclosures,* and other NCLC publications.

**Rent-to-Own Transactions.** Rent-to-Own (RTO) businesses are essentially appliance and furniture retailers which arrange lease agreements for those customers who cannot purchase goods with cash. The agreements contain purchase options that typically allow the lessees to obtain title to the goods by making a nominal payment at the end of a short term, such as 18 months. In addition, the leases are short term, so that the "rental payments" are due weekly or monthly.

The RTO industry aims its marketing efforts primarily at low-income consumers by advertising in ethnic media, public transportation, and in public housing projects. The sales pitch suggests that RTO has many attractive features: no credit checks, quick delivery, weekly payments, no or small down payments, quick repair service, and no harm to one's credit rating if the transaction is canceled.

In fact, many of these RTO "leases" are disguised sales made at astronomic and undisclosed effective interest rates.

For example:

> - A consumer rents a 19-inch color TV ($300 value)
> - He pays $16/week x 52 weeks = $832
>
> $832 paid –
> $300 (value of the TV) =
> _____
> $532 (254% interest on an annual basis).

In nearly every state, there are RTO statutes that insulate dealers from most consumer abuse claims. Nevertheless, legal handles still exist to catch some of the more egregious practices of RTO dealers. For more information, see NCLC's manuals, *The Cost of Credit: Regulation and Legal Challenges*, *Repossessions and Foreclosures*, and other NCLC publications.

**Tax Refund Anticipation Loans**. Tax refund anticipation loans involve cash advanced against the consumer's expected tax refund. They are generally available through tax preparers. However, a used car dealer or two and some retail merchants near tribal reservations have been known to engage in this practice. Most refund lending is now performed by major depository institutions, including bank subsidiaries of major finance companies, through local tax preparers.

Refund lenders require the consumer to file a tax return with the IRS electronically. The consumer pays a fee for the filing, typically in the range of $20 to $60. The electronic filing cuts the time the consumer waits for the refund in half. . .to two or three weeks. The refund loan puts cash into the consumer's hand in two or three days, which accounts for its appeal as a quick and "painless" way to get cash. Often, the lender does not explain the shorter waiting period due to electronic filing.

The loan amount is the refund minus the loan fee, the tax preparation fee, and the electronic filing fee. Loan fees are typically flat fees, set on a sliding scale based on the amount of the expected refund. The fees charged translate into APRs of well over 100%.

Aside from the fees that eat into a consumer's tax refund, consumers who are entitled to the earned income tax credit are hit especially hard. The purpose of the earned income tax credit is to augment the income of wage earners at the lowest end of the economic spectrum. More information on these loans can be found in NCLC's *Cost of Credit* manual.[2]

# ALTERNATIVE SOURCES OF CREDIT

Educating consumers to avoid high cost lending is difficult when there are few (or no) alternatives available. For this reason, it is critical for advocates to learn more about alternative, less expensive sources of credit in their communities and to help direct clients to these resources. Credit unions, including many community development institutions, often offer small loans at reasonable rates. More information about community development credit unions is available from the Coalition of Community Development Financial Institutions, 215-923-5363, http://www.cdfi.org and the National Federation of Community Development Credit Unions, 212-809-1850, http://www.natfed.org. In addition, many immigrant communities have developed community-based lending services. For example, many communities have set up rotating credit associations where groups pool their funds and then rotate the pool around the group until all members have received it. These rotating pools are known by a variety of ethnic names such as "kye" in the Korean community, "ekub" in the Ethiopian community, "esusu" in the West Indies community and "hui" in the Chinese or Vietnamese communities.[3]

---

[1] For more information, see NCLC's manual, *The Cost of Credit* § 2.3.3.9 (2d ed. 2000 and Supp).

[2] *See The Cost of Credit,* §7.5.4.1.

[3] For more information about community-based lending and informal lending networks, see Lan Cao, "Looking at Communities and Markets," 74 Notre Dame L. Rev. 841 (March 1999).

# 5

# CASHING CHECKS AND OPENING BANK ACCOUNTS

---

- *Bank Accounts: How to Help Immigrants Save Money and Avoid Theft*
- *If an Immigrant Is Turned Down for a Bank Account*
- *Helping Undocumented Immigrants Open Bank Accounts*
- *Electronic Receipt of Benefits*

---

## BANK ACCOUNTS: HOW TO HELP IMMIGRANTS SAVE MONEY AND AVOID THEFT

Even though many consumers, particularly newcomers to the United States, may be suspicious of banks, it is important to help them understand the benefits of bank checking and savings accounts. If an immigrant is not using a bank account to cash checks and pay bills, chances are she is spending too much for these services. Check cashing outlets will cash government, employer, or personal checks, but at a high cost.

For example:

---

- A consumer's weekly payroll check is $320
- The check casher charges her 2% of the check's face value to cash it ($6.40)
- The consumer cashes 50 of these checks per year

$320 x .02 (2% fee) = $6.40/week
$6.40 x 50 weeks = **$320 each year for check cashing services**

---

This example and more advice on opening a bank account are available for consumers in NCLC's brochure, "Cashing Checks and Opening Bank Accounts" (in English, Spanish, Chinese, Korean, Vietnamese and Russian – see the order form in the back of this Handbook at Appendix 1).

In addition to spending too much on fees, immigrants who use check cashers are often targeted by robbers. For example, four immigrants in Austin, Texas were murdered by robbers who targeted the undocumented. The robbers knew that undocumented workers carry a large amount of cash on payday due to lack of bank accounts.[1]

If an immigrant feels that a bank checking account is not right for him, there are a number of alternatives, including:

- Credit Unions;

- Community Development Credit Unions;

- Low-cost electronic bank accounts (these accounts offer ATM access but not check-writing privileges).

One advantage of credit unions in certain states is that they offer their members relatively inexpensive ways to send money overseas. Information on this program is included in Chapter 8, "Money Wire Transfers." Also, some credit unions have been encouraged to make accounts available to undocumented immigrants.

# IF AN IMMIGRANT IS TURNED DOWN FOR A BANK ACCOUNT

Advocates should help clients who are turned down for bank accounts to find out why. Some banks deny accounts to people who have bounced checks in the past. If the decision was based on the bank's review of a credit report, the consumer has a right to a free copy of the report within 60 days of the denial. At some banks, problems with past credit history can be explained to a manager or other bank employee. For more information on credit histories, see Chapter 11, "Credit Reporting."

# HELPING UNDOCUMENTED IMMIGRANTS OPEN BANK ACCOUNTS

Undocumented immigrants often have a hard time opening bank accounts, but it is not impossible. Usually, banks will ask for a Social Security Number (SSN) to open a bank account, because they need to report interest on the account as income to the Internal Revenue Service. However, there are several ways an undocumented immigrant can open a bank account without a SSN:

**Open a Non-Interest Bearing Account.** A bank may let an immigrant open an account without a SSN if the account does not pay interest, because the bank will not need to deal with taxes on interest income. One bank has a "no-frills" electronic ATM-only account that it is making available specifically for undocumented customers. Note that even if a bank allows an undocumented immigrant to open a non-interesting bearing account without a SSN, the bank will still require one or more forms of identification, such as a passport or driver's license.

**ITIN.** A second alternative is to open a bank account by using an Individual Taxpayer Identification Number (ITIN) instead of a SSN. The ITIN is issued by the Internal Revenue Service, and is used for tax purposes to identify aliens who are not eligible for a SSN. An ITIN has the same 9 digit sequence as a SSN, but begins with the number 9 (i.e., 9XX-XX-XXXX). *The IRS has specifically stated that an undocumented* *immigrant may obtain an ITIN.* The ITIN is not valid for employment and does not confer any immigration status on the recipient.

In order to get an ITIN, an immigrant will need to fill out an IRS Form W-7. She needs to prove her identity and that she is a foreign national. This can be shown with a foreign passport, driver's license, or other documents. The IRS requires originals, but an immigrant can go to a local IRS office or "Acceptance Agent" to apply for the ITIN. For a list of Acceptance Agents, go to www.irs.ustreas.gov/prod/ind_info/agents.html.

In addition to the ITIN, the banks will require the immigrant to complete a tax form, most probably an IRS-W8BEN.

**Opening a Joint Account with a Legal Resident or Citizen.**
Many undocumented immigrants have family members or friends who are legal resident or citizens. These immigrants can open a joint account with the legal resident as the primary account holder, using that person's SSN. Since the joint account holder will have free access to the money in the account, the undocumented immigrant should be warned about the risks of this alternative, and be advised to choose a joint account holder whom she can trust.

# ELECTRONIC RECEIPT OF BENEFITS

The federal and state governments are increasingly using electronic methods to deliver public assistance benefits. For some immigrants, this trend makes getting a bank account even more important. Immigrants will also need to understand how to use an ATM and store card readers.

Most recipients now receive food stamps benefits on an electronic card, and all food stamps will be delivered electronically by October 2002. Many states have also decided to pay cash assistance electronically using the same systems. Many recipients of federal benefits, including Social Security or SSI, will soon be receiving their benefits electronically.

**Special ETA Accounts.** In order to implement electronic delivery of federal benefits, the federal government has developed a special low-cost bank account called the "electronic transfer account" (ETA).

An ETA costs $3.00 per month or less and allows four (4) free withdrawals. Depending on the bank, the recipient can make these free withdrawals from a teller, ATM, or both. Additional withdrawals or withdrawals from certain ATMs may cost a fee. To locate a bank or credit union that offers ETAs, call 1-888-382-3311 or go to www.eta-find.gov. ETAs are only available to Social Security, SSI, and other federal benefits recipients.

**Hardship Waivers.** Recipients can still receive federal payments by check if getting an electronic payment would cause a hardship. Valid reasons for a waiver include *inability to read or speak English*, financial reasons, disability, or geographic barriers. Most importantly, if a recipient does not sign up for direct deposit to a bank account or open an ETA, she will continue to receive paper checks.

---

[1] Janet Jacobs, "Working To Stop Crime, En Espanol," Austin-American Statesman, June 4, 2001, B1.

# 6

# CRITICAL CONSUMER LAW PROTECTIONS

- *Critical Consumer Law Protections Specifically for Immigrants and Non-English Speakers*
- *General Consumer Law Protections*

## CRITICAL CONSUMER LAW PROTECTIONS SPECIFICALLY FOR IMMIGRANTS AND NON-ENGLISH SPEAKERS

Below is a summary of general consumer protection laws as well as laws that specifically apply to immigrants and non-English speakers. A number of other laws and statutes are discussed throughout this handbook. For example, laws related to automobile issues are discussed in the "Used Car Fraud" chapter and student loan laws and regulations are covered in the "Student Loans" chapter.

**Laws Requiring Non-English Translations of Contracts.**[1]
A few states require businesses to give consumers translations of contracts if they negotiate (or in some cases advertise) in other languages. The laws vary by state. In some states, the statute applies only to specific types of transactions such as rent-to-own sales. Translations may be required in any language in which negotiations occurred or only in a specific language such as Spanish.

States with contract translation statutes include:

- **Arizona**: Ariz. Rev. Stat. § 44-1797.05 (applies to discount buying services)
  Ariz. Rev. Stat. § 44-5004 (applies to door-to-door sales)

- **California**: Cal. Civ. Code § 1632 (applies to Spanish only)

- **Florida**: Florida Rules of the Department of Legal Affairs, ch. 2-9.05 (Advertising and Sales)
  Fla. Stat. Ann. § 636.015 (prepaid limited health services organizations)
  Fla. Stat. Ann. § 641.305 (health maintenance organizations)
  Fla. Stat. Ann. § 641.421 (prepaid health clinics)

- **Illinois**: 815 Ill. Comp. Stat. Ann. § 505/2N (applies to all retail transactions, except for transactions made with a credit card)

- **Nebraska**: Neb. Rev. Stat. § 69-1604 (door-to-door sales -- notice of cancellation rights)

- **New Jersey**: N.J. Stat. Ann. § 17.16C-61.6 and - 100 (retail installment sales)

- **New Mexico**: N.M Stat. Ann. § 57-26-4 (rent-to-own)

- **Oregon**: Or. Rev. Stat. § 646.249 (lease-purchase agreements)

- **Pennsylvania**: Pa. Stat. Ann. tit. 73, § 201-7 (door-to-door sales)

- **Texas**: Tex. Bus. + Com. Code Ann. § 35.72 (rent-to-own)

- **Vermont**: Vt. Stat. Ann. tit. 9, § 2454 (door-to-door sales)

- **Wisconsin**: Wisconsin Dep't of Agriculture, Trade and Consumer Protection Rules Wis. Ad. Code ch. ATCP 127, Home Solicitation Selling (applies to door-to-door sales)

Wis. Stat. § 423.203 (notice of cancellation rights)

- **Wyoming**: Wyo. Stat. An. § 40-19-106 (rent-to-own)

**The FTC Used Car Rule.**[2] The FTC Used Car Rule requires disclosure of certain information in the sale of used cars. When a sale is conducted in Spanish, the Buyers Guide and the contract language disclosures must be available in both Spanish and English.[3] In addition, if a dealer offers to sell vehicles to some consumers who speak only Spanish and others who speak English, the dealer must display both an English and a Spanish Buyers Guide before the vehicle is offered for sale.

# GENERAL CONSUMER LAW PROTECTIONS

**Unfair and Deceptive Acts and Practices Statutes.** Every state and the District of Columbia has at least one broad consumer protection statute that falls into the general category of an unfair and deceptive acts and practices statute (UDAP). These laws are discussed in detail in NCLC's manual *Unfair and Deceptive Acts and Practices.*

There are many advantages to using UDAP statutes to challenge abusive, deceptive, and unfair marketplace transactions, including:

- UDAP statutes are very broad, allowing advocates to challenge a wide range of abusive behavior that may or may not violate another state or federal civil or criminal statute.

- Almost every state UDAP statute allows consumers to file private lawsuits. In most states, clients can seek many different types of relief in UDAP claims, including actual, treble, minimum and/ or punitive damages, injunctive relief to stop abusive practices, class actions, and in most states, attorney fees as well. The type of relief available varies by state.

- Most UDAP statutes provide for private injunction actions. This is a very powerful remedy, allowing consumers to seek a court-ordered injunction to prevent a seller from engaging in specific types of misconduct or abusive practices. A seller may treat occasional damage awards as a cost of doing business, but an injunction can eliminate the seller's use of the challenged practice against all future customers.

- UDAP statutes do not usually require proof of a seller's intent or knowledge of a deceptive or unfair business practice. Sellers cannot simply defend a lawsuit by claiming that they acted in good faith.

- Most UDAP statutes do not require proof that consumers relied to their detriment on the seller's misrepresentation or abusive practice.

---

[1] *See generally* Steven W. Bender, "Consumer Protection for Latinos: Overcoming Language Fraud and English-Only in the Marketplace," 45 Am. U.L. Rev. 1027 (April 1996).

[2] For more information on used car issues, see Chapter 10, "Used Car Fraud."

[3] 16 C.F.R. § 455.5.

# 7

# *NOTARIO* AND IMMIGRATION CONSULTANT FRAUD

---

- *Typical Scams*
- *Summary of Legal Remedies to Challenge Immigration Consultant Fraud*
- *Preventing Fraud*

---

The number of scam artists preying upon immigrants seeking assistance in obtaining legal residence work authorization, or citizenship has risen dramatically in recent years. Many unscrupulous consultants claim that they are attorneys or that they have close connections to the Immigration and Naturalization Service (INS). Others use titles such as notary public or *notario* to deceive people into believing that they are lawyers. In many Spanish-speaking countries, a *notario* is an attorney, often possessing more credentials than other lawyers.

In many areas, honest and responsible immigration consultants provide a real service. Unfortunately, there are almost always dishonest consultants, and frequently dishonest attorneys as well. Victims of these scams not only lose large sums of money but also are likely to suffer serious harm to their immigration status.

There are a number of reasons why immigrants are targeted. Many new immigrants feel a sense of desperation about their immigration status. Their dreams of permanent residency in the United States often lead them to believe the outrageous claims of unscrupulous consultants. The problem is compounded by the lack of affordable legal services nationwide. To make matters worse, many legal aid offices are barred from helping certain categories of immigrants. The few organizations that do exist are often overwhelmed with requests for help.

## TYPICAL SCAMS

Those seeking to adjust their legal status or obtain work authorization in the United States are often bewildered by the complex immigration laws in this country. Frequent changes and adjustments in these programs make understanding immigration law even more difficult. Unscrupulous immigration consultants take advantage of these circumstances in many different ways.

Typical scams include:

- Charging exorbitant fees for immigration services and then failing to file any documents.

- Filing false asylum claims on behalf of victims who do not speak or read English and have no idea what the application contains.

- Charging fees to prepare applications for nonexistent immigration programs or for legitimate programs for which the immigrant does not qualify, such as asylum or labor certification.

## SUMMARY OF LEGAL REMEDIES TO CHALLENGE IMMIGRATION CONSULTANT FRAUD

Many states have enacted statutes regulating immigration consultants. Most of these statutes exempt accredited representatives. An accredited representative is a non-attorney working for an organization accredited by the Board of Immigration Appeals. Non-attorneys who work for nonprofit agencies or law school legal clinics are also generally exempt from state immigration consultant statutes. All of these state laws prohibit immigration consultants from providing legal assistance. Several specify limited services that the consultant may lawfully perform.

The following is a current list of state immigration consultant statutes:

- **Arizona** Ariz. Rev. Stat. Ann. §§ 12-2701 to 12-2703

- **California.** Cal. Bus. & Prof Code § 22440-44

- **Illinois.** 815 Ill. Comp. Stat. § 505/2AA

- **Minnesota.** Minn. Stat. § 325E.031

- **New Jersey.** N.J. Stat. Ann. § 2C:21-31

- **New Mexico.** N.M. Stat. Ann. §§ 36-3-1 to 36-3-10

- **Washington.** Wash. Rev. Code §§ 19.154.010 to 19.154.902

A few cities have also passed regulations or ordinances dealing with immigration consultant fraud.

Other statutes to consider in challenging immigration consultant fraud include state unfair and deceptive acts and practices (UDAP) statutes, state statutes prohibiting the unauthorized practice of law, and state contract translation statutes. Common law claims, such as fraud and breach of contract, may also be used.

## PREVENTING FRAUD

Immigration consultant fraud occurs largely because there is a lack of affordable legal assistance in this country. As long as low-income people have difficulty accessing the legal system, there will likely be nonattorneys vying for their business. Not all immigration consultants are rip-off artists, and in some cases clients feel more comfortable doing business with them. Too often, however, the consultants lack the required skills and/ or intentionally aim to rip off unsuspecting consumers.

One important solution to the problem of nonattorney scams is to continue to advocate for expansions in free or sliding scale legal services and pro bono commitments.  For information about available free legal resources in immigration matters, see http://www.usdoj.gov/eoir/probono/states.htm.

There are also preventative steps that clients and their advocates can take, including:

1.  Contacting local and state regulatory agencies (usually bar organizations) to check whether legal providers claiming to be attorneys are in fact licensed to practice law.

2.  Working with law enforcement to encourage criminal prosecution of offenders.

3.  Advising clients of their rights when using nonattorney services, including:

    - In most cases, a right to receive a written contract (and in many cases three days to cancel those contracts);

    - In many cases, a right to a translated copy of the contract;

    - In many cases, a right to a contract explicitly stating in bold letters that the provider is not an attorney.

To get a copy of NCLC's consumer education brochure on immigration consultant fraud, send in the order form included at the Appendix 3 or download the brochure from NCLC's web site, http://www.nclc.org/osi/index.htm.

# 8

# MONEY WIRE TRANSFERS

---

- *How to Help Immigrants Avoid Fraud and Save Money*
- *Addressing Money Wire Transfer Fraud*
- *Saving on Money Wire Transfer Fees*

---

## How to Help Immigrants Avoid Fraud and Save Money

One of the most significant contributions of immigrants in the U.S. is the substantial amount of money they send to their families and others in their countries of origins. Many of these immigrants use money wire transfer services in the U.S. to send this money. Yet fees and hidden costs charged for wire transfers can be expensive, ranging from 10 to 25% or more of the amount of money sent. In addition, the businesses that offer these services often sell other costly and fringe financial services, such as check cashing or payday loans.

Even more disturbing, sometimes immigrants give money to questionable wire transfer services that never send the money to the intended recipient. Here are a few ways to protect immigrants from fraud and to help them save money in fees.

## Addressing Money Wire Transfer Fraud

The money wire transfer industry is primarily regulated by the states. About 28 states and the District of Columbia have laws requiring businesses that sell money wire transfer services (also called "money transmitters") to be licensed by the state banking agency. Some of these states have laws specifically requiring licensing of money transmitters who send money to foreign countries.[1]

You can check with your state banking agency to determine if you are in a state that requires licensing, and check whether a specific money wire transfer business has a license. (The website of the Money Transmitter Regulators Association, a group of state banking officials, has a list of useful links to state banking agencies that regulate money transmitters.   See www.mtraweb.org.)   When using an unfamiliar money wire transfer business in a state that requires licensing, always make sure the business is licensed.

Consumers who lose money to shady money wire operations should file a complaint with their state banking agency. Most of the states which require licensing also require money transmitters to post a bond or other security.   If an immigrant loses money to a money transmitter that is licensed and bonded, the bond may be a potential source to recover the lost funds if the transmitter goes out of business. New York State even has an insurance fund to reimburse money wire fraud victims.

## Saving on Money Wire Transfer Fees

Even if a money wire transfer business is licensed and reputable, there is always the possibility of a problem in transmission.   Consumers should be aware of the refund and loss provisions in a wire transfer contract.   They should always save their receipts in case there is a problem, and keep on eye on any time limits for filing a refund claim.

For other immigrants, the money sent by a wire transfer will arrive safely, but a significant chunk of it will be lost to fees.   Some of these fees can be "hidden" in the form of lower than normal exchange rates. As a result of a class action settlement in December 2000, Western Union and Money Gram agreed to disclose to consumers the existence and amount of the difference between the exchange rates they give customers and the prevailing rate, also called the "spread."[2]

The bottom line is that immigrants should always ask about the currency exchange rate if they don't see it posted. To avoid hefty fees, they should shop around for both the best fee and exchange rate. There are a number of lower cost alternatives to traditional money wire services, especially for sending money to Mexico. Credit unions in a number of states offer low cost money wire transfers to credit unions in over 40 countries under the IRnet program from the World Council of Credit Unions (WOCCU). For more information on IRnet, see the WOCCU's website at www.woccu.org.[3] The U.S. Post Office has introduced a program called *Dinero Seguro*, which offers money wire transfers from post offices in California, Illinois and Texas. Finally, the Mexican government is looking into ways to introduce even lower cost alternatives, such as a system of ATMs that can be used by both immigrants and their families in Mexico.[4]

To get a copy of NCLC's consumer education brochure on money wire transfers, send in the order form included at Appendix 3 or download the brochure from NCLC's web site, http://www.nclc.org/osi/index.htm. For more information on money wire transfers, see NCLC's manual *Consumer Banking and Payments Law* (2001) § 2.2.

---

[1] California and Massachusetts. California's statute specifically states that it regulates foreign wire transfers to protect the "large and diverse population many of whom are concerned with the financial plight of people remaining in the countries which they left." California Financial Code, § 1800(b).

[2] In Re Mexico Money Transfer Litigation, 2000 U.S. Dist. LEXIS 18,863 (N.D. Ill. December 21, 2000). This settlement was criticized for, among other things, not prohibiting or limiting the amount that Western Union and Money Gram could charge for the spread, and for providing consumer recovery in the form of coupons.

[3] The IRnet program is limited to credit union members, but many of these credit unions focus on serving underserved communities, including immigrants. If immigrants can become a member of the credit union, an added benefit of using IRnet is that they will become more familiar with using a mainstream financial institution. According to WOCCU, credit unions can serve undocumented immigrants in their field of membership. See www.woccu.org.

[4] Wells Fargo already offers a service called Intercuenta Express in which customers can deposit money with that bank and have it withdrawn from ATM machines in Mexico.

# 9

# AFFIDAVIT OF SUPPORT

Another area that is likely to have far-reaching consumer consequences for immigrants is the new affidavit of support form. The affidavit of support and sponsorship requirements enacted by the 1996 immigration law have been in place since December 1997, but the ramifications are still being felt. The new affidavit of support form requires most immigrants to submit affidavits of support from sponsors in order to gain admission to the United States.[1] A copy of the form is reprinted at Appendix 2.

The form requires the sponsor to support the immigrant at an annual income of at least 125 percent of the federal poverty line. This support obligation includes reimbursement of agencies (public or private) that pay public means-tested benefits to the immigrant during the time of the sponsor's support obligation. Sponsors also may face lawsuits from the immigrants themselves if they fail to support them at the required level.

A wide range of consumer law issues is likely to arise in this area. First, some questions may be raised about the enforceability of the new form by agencies and/or by sponsored immigrants. If the form is enforceable, sponsors will need assistance in defending collection lawsuits and later in dealing with collection methods such as wage garnishment. Second, creditors such as landlords may attempt to pursue sponsors for other obligations that are incurred by sponsored immigrants that arguably relate to their support.

The affidavit of support issue may cause conflicts among different immigrant clients. Some may be sponsoring relatives and seeking to avoid liability, while others may be sponsored immigrants seeking to enforce support. For more information on this issue, see Catholic

Legal Immigration Network, National Immigration Law Center, *Affidavit of Support Requirements: A Practitioner's Guide* (1998).[2]

As of 2000, there have been little or no reports of government benefit granting agencies seeking repayment from sponsors. However, many immigrants have reported that they would not even try to apply due to fears that it would affect their immigration status or that their sponsors would face consequences.

There are a number of good resources to keep up on developments, including:

- The National Immigration Law Center (http://www.nilc.org); 213-639-3900.

- Catholic Legal Immigration Network (http://www.cliniclegal.org); 202-635-2556.

- U.S. State Department's Bureau of Consular Affairs has a web site that provides guidance on completing the form, http://travel.state.gov/aos.html.

---

[1]  62 Fed. Reg. 54346 (Oct. 20, 1997).  Final regulations pending at time of publication.  The INS has published numerous memos and clarifications since 1997.  For more information, contact the National Immigration Law Center at 213-639-3900 or visit NILC's web site at http://www.nilc.org.

[2]  Available from CLINIC, 415 Michigan Ave., NE, Washington, D.C. 20017.

# 10

# USED CAR FRAUD

- *Types of Scams*
- *Other Protections*
- *Car Repossessions*

For many immigrants the transition from public assistance to work translates into a heightened need for transportation and the purchase of a car. This opens the door to potential abuses by used-car dealers and high-rate lenders and to other car-related consumer problems.

An astonishing percentage of car sales involve fraud, deception, or unfair conduct. Consumer claims can arise at every step of the sales process, including when:

- the consumer shows up at the car dealer;

- the consumer enters into negotiations with a salesperson;

- the consumer signs documents to purchase a car;

- the car breaks down;

- the consumer stops paying for the financing of the car;

- the car is repossessed and disposed of by the creditor; or

- the consumer is sued for a deficiency balance.

A summary of these practices and legal challenges is presented below.

# TYPES OF SCAMS

**Odometer Fraud.** One type of odometer fraud involves tampering with an odometer so that its reading is less than the car's actual mileage. Another type is failing to disclose that an odometer has exceeded its mechanical limits (for example, when a car has really traveled 150,000 miles, not the 50,000 shown on the odometer). In addition to state UDAP statutes and common law theories, there is a federal odometer act and many state odometer laws that can be used to challenge odometer fraud[1].

**Salvage Fraud.** A car is considered "salvage" if it has been declared a total loss because of a car collision, flooding, fire, or other serious physical accident. Many unscrupulous dealers patch up these cars and sell them to unsuspecting customers without disclosing the salvage history. Millions of these cars are still on the road.

There are many challenges to this practice including state salvage statutes and state statutes requiring disclosure of wreck damage for certain used cars. Advocates can also challenge the sale of cars that were severely wrecked, even if the damage is short of being declared salvage[2].

**Lemon Laws**. Lemon laws generally require car manufacturers to repair problems, and to refund the consumer's money or replace the vehicle if problems cannot be repaired. In a few states, lemon laws also cover used cars[3].

**Lemon Laundering**. Lemon laundering involves a manufacturer buying back a lemon car from a consumer, then passing on that car to another consumer without its lemon history being disclosed. Among other challenges, state unfair and deceptive acts and practices (UDAP) statutes can be used against dealers engaging in lemon laundering, as well as state lemon laundering statutes that specifically require title branding and other disclosures[4].

**Misrepresentation of Number or Nature of Prior Users.**
Related misrepresentations concern the nature of the prior use. For
example, many consumers would want to know, but many dealers fail
to disclose, if a car had previously been a rental car, police car, taxi cab,
or lease car, and whether it had been repossessed.

Car dealers may misrepresent the number of prior owners. A
typical representation is that the car was traded into the dealer by
someone who took excellent care of it since purchasing it new. In fact,
the car may have had a number of consumer owners, and could also
have been passed between a number of dealers, wholesalers, and
auctions.

**Stolen Vehicles and Defective Titles.** A car sold to a
consumer can have a defective title for any number of reasons. One is
that the car is stolen or the vehicle identification number is fictitious.
Another is that pre-existing liens are not satisfied or that the title was
never transferred to the consumer. Sale of a car with defective title
presents the consumer with a number of special legal claims.

# OTHER PROTECTIONS

The FTC Used Car Rule requires disclosure of certain information in
the sale of used cars.[5] When a sale is conducted in Spanish, the Buyers
Guide and the contract language disclosures must be available in both
Spanish and English.[6] In addition, if a dealer offers to sell vehicles to
some consumers who speak only Spanish and others who speak
English, the dealer must display both an English and a Spanish Buyers
Guide before the vehicle is offered for sale.

# CAR REPOSSESSIONS

All too often a client does not seek legal help until the client's car is
about to be repossessed, or, worse, already seized. A detailed
discussion of how to help clients at each stage of the repossession
process can be found in the National Consumer Law Center's manual,
*Repossessions and Foreclosures* (4th ed. 1999 & Supp.). A wide range of
consumer warranty and fraud defenses can be raised to revoke
acceptance prior to repossession of a used car, to prevent or reduce a

deficiency after repossession, and as sales-related claims in deficiency actions.

---

[1] The federal odometer act is codified at 49 U.S.C. §§ 32701-32711. Many states also have their own odometer laws. For information on these state laws, see National Consumer Law Center, Automobile Fraud App. C (1998 and Supp.).

[2] For a listing of state laws, see NCLC, Automobile Fraud App. C (1998 and Supp.).

[3] For new car lemon law issues, see National Consumer Law Center, Consumer Warranty Law Ch. 13 (2d ed. 2001). For used cars, see Warranty manual Ch. 14. To date, the following states have used car lemon laws: Hawaii, Massachusetts, Minnesota, New Jersey, New York, and Rhode Island.

[4] National Consumer Law Center, Automobile Fraud App. C (1998 and Supp.).

[5] 16 C.F.R. § 455.

[6] 16 C.F.R. § 455.5.

# 11

# CREDIT REPORTING

- *How to Order Credit Reports*
- *What to Look for in a Credit Report*
- *Who Can Review a Credit Report?*
- *Credit Repair Scams*
- *Identity Theft*

A credit report is a record of how an individual has borrowed and repaid debts. Creditors usually look at this report to decide whether or not to grant credit.

It is a good idea to help clients keep track of credit histories by ordering reports. This is the first step in deciding how to deal with problems with a credit history. There are three major credit reporting bureaus. Consumers should be advised to order a report from all three.

## HOW TO ORDER CREDIT REPORTS

Equifax
P.O. Box 740241
Atlanta, GA  30374
800-685-1111
http://www.equifax.com

Experian
National Consumers Assistance Center
P.O. Box 2002

Allen, TX 75013
888-397-3742
http://www.experian.com

Trans Union
Consumer Disclosure Center
P.O. Box 1000
Chester, PA  19022
800-888-4213
http://www.tuc.com

Sample reports are available on-line at the credit bureau web sites. These addresses are current as of October 2001.

# WHAT TO LOOK FOR IN A CREDIT REPORT?

Consumers should at least look for the following possible problems:

**Are there any errors?**  If there is an error, consumers should fill out a dispute form or write a letter explaining the problem.  The agency must then investigate and get back to consumers, usually within thirty days.  The agency must notify the consumer within five days of completing the investigation and must include a copy of the credit report if it has been revised.  If the problem is not resolved, consumers may file a written statement (sometimes limited to 100 words) explaining their side of the story.

## Is There Any Old Information?

Look for:

- Credit information older than 7 years.
- Bankruptcy information older than 10 years.

This is considered "old" information and should no longer be in a credit report.

# WHO CAN REVIEW A CREDIT REPORT?

The federal Fair Credit Reporting Act (15 U.S.C. § 1681 and following) and state credit reporting laws have rules about who can look at a consumer's credit report and how the report may be used. If the use of the report does not fit within those that the Act explicitly allows, the use is impermissible.

Some of the most important people who can request credit reports (with limited exceptions) include:

- **Employers**
  **Exception:**Employers must first get written authorization from employees and prospective employees and give certain disclosures.

- **Government Agencies**
  **Exception:**Not all government agencies can look at consumer credit reports. For example, district attorneys cannot look at reports to investigate criminal or civil cases and the Immigration and Naturalization Service (INS) cannot get a report for an immigration proceeding or for reviewing citizenship applications.

- **Insurance Companies**

- **Judgment Creditors**

- **Potential Creditors**

- **Landlords and Mortgage Lenders**

Credit reports are less important in other types of transactions such as:

- **Utilities**
  Most utility companies focus only on whether a consumer owes money to that particular company.

- **Student Loans and Grants**
  However, borrowers who are in default on student loans can't get new ones until they get out of default.

- **Divorce, Child Custody and Immigration Proceedings**
  Government agencies are allowed to look at credit reports in these cases only if they get a special court order.

# CREDIT REPAIR SCAMS

Many low-income consumers feel desperate to "fix" their credit reports. These consumers, including many immigrants, can be the targets of unscrupulous credit repair agencies that very rarely offer valuable services, and are often outright scams. Clients should be advised to beware of these common erroneous claims made by credit repair companies.

**"We can erase bad credit"**
The truth is that no one can erase bad credit information from a report if it is accurate.

**"Only we can remove old or inaccurate information"**
The truth is that if there are legitimate errors on a report or old information, consumers can correct the report themselves for free.

**"The bad information on your report is accurate but we'll erase it anyway"**
The truth is that if this means lying to the credit reporting agency, it is illegal.

There is a federal Credit Repair Organizations Act (CROA) and many states have laws that can be used to challenge the abusive practices of credit repair agencies. The CROA requires credit repair agencies to provide certain disclosures to consumers prior to executing agreements. Contracts to repair credit must also contain certain terms. In addition, consumers must be given notice of their three day right to cancel the contract for any reason.[1] Additional protections for credit reporting problems can be found in the federal Fair Credit Reporting Act and state statutes.[2]

# IDENTITY THEFT

Identity theft is a growing problem across the country. Immigrants may have problems with stolen identities particularly if they were previously undocumented and worked using different social security numbers. Others may have names that confuse credit bureaus, leading the bureaus to mix up various files. Unfortunately, in other cases, identity thieves deliberately steal identities.

The consequences can be devastating. Identity thieves can obtain loans, open credit accounts, rent apartments, and buy cars or other products all in the victim's name. It is frighteningly easy for thieves to steal an identity. Some of the ways they operate include:

- Stealing wallets;

- Filling out a change-of-address form and collecting the victim's mail;

- Stealing pre-approved credit offers from the trash;

- Looking over the victim's shoulder at ATMs to gather PIN numbers; or

- Using personal information that was shared on the Internet.

One of the best ways to prevent this crime is through education. Consumers should learn to keep their private information secure. One of the simplest ways to protect against identity theft is to buy a paper shredder and use it to shred important documents such as credit card bills and credit card offers.

The federal government and most states now have tougher criminal laws designed to fight identity theft, but it is a difficult crime to catch. For more information, check out the Federal Trade Commission web site http://www.ftc.gov and the Social Security

Administration web site http://www.ssa.gov. Victims should also call Social Security to report any fraudulent use of their SSN. In addition, victims should file a complaint with the FTC by contacting the FTC's Identity Theft Hotline 1-877-IDTHEFT or by mail: Identity Theft Clearinghouse, Federal Trade Commission, 600 Pennsylvania Ave., NW, Washington, D.C. 20580, www.consumer.gov/idtheft. The FTC cannot bring criminal cases but they can give information about how to resolve the problems that result from identity theft.

Victims should also contact the three main credit bureaus Equifax (800-525-6285), Experian (888-397-3742), and Trans Union (800-680-7289). They can add a fraud alert to victims' credit reports as well as a victim's statement asking that creditors call before opening any new accounts or changing existing accounts.

---

[1] 15 U.S.C. §§1679-1679j. For more information, see National Consumer Law Center, Fair Credit Reporting Act Ch. 8 (4th ed. 1998 and Supp.).

[2] Federal Fair Credit Reporting Act: 15 U.S.C. §§ 1681-1681u.

# 12

# TELEPHONE AND UTILITY ISSUES

- *Telephone Issues*
- *Utility Assistance for Low-Income Families*
- *Helping an Immigrant Fight a Termination of Service*

## TELEPHONE ISSUES

For recent immigrants, staying in touch with loved ones in their countries of origin is an important but sometimes expensive activity. One of the most helpful ways to assist an immigrant minimize expenses is to review his phone bills and see if you can find a cheaper international calling plan. In selecting a long distance plan, pay attention to any monthly fees, minimum charges, time restrictions, and other fine print.

Telecommunications companies often focus their marketing activities on immigrants, because immigrants are a very lucrative segment of the market. Unfortunately, this heightened attention on immigrants occurs with both legitimate and not-so-legitimate companies and activities.

**Phone Slamming.** Phone slamming is the switching of long distance phone service without the consumer's knowledge or consent. Sometimes this switching happens by mistake, but often phone companies "trick" consumers into signing up for different services. These companies send out contest entry forms, checks or surveys that authorize the switch in fine print. Other companies train their telemarketers to make confusing offers. Phone companies often hire bilingual telemarketers to sell phone services, and some of these telemarketers may engage in slamming of immigrants.

Phone slamming is illegal. Under federal law, consumers are not required to pay the slammer for any calls they've made within the first 30 days after they have been slammed. After the first 30 days, they are only required to pay for charges their preferred carrier would have charged.

Advice on what to tell an immigrant who has been slammed is included in the National Consumer Law Center's brochure "Stop Phone Slamming" (available in English, Spanish, Chinese, Korean, and Russian – see the order form at Appendix 3).

You may wish to help an immigrant who has been slammed to file a complaint with the Federal Communications Commission. The FCC's toll-free complaint number is 1-888-CALL-FCC (1-888-225-5322). Written complaints can be sent to FCC, Common Carrier Bureau Enforcement Division, Washington, D.C. 20554. You also have the option of filing a complaint with the FCC via the Internet at www.fcc.gov/ccb/enforce/index-complaints.html. Even if the company that slammed the immigrant properly drops all charges, you may wish to inform the FCC of unauthorized switches that are targeting your community.

**Pre-Paid Phone Cards.** Pre-paid phone cards represent telephone time a consumer buys in advance. Phone cards are one of the fastest growing segments in the telecommunications industry. Immigrants are major users of phone cards, and many phone card companies specially market to one or two ethnic immigrant communities. Unfortunately, phone card fraud and problems with phone cards are also a significant consumer problem in these communities. Because immigrants pay up-front, they are often out of pocket - and out of luck - if they discover a problem trying to use the card.

Most phone cards work using a toll-free access telephone number and a personal identification number (PIN). The phone card companies have computers that use the PIN to keep track of card usage - how much phone time is left in minutes or units. Some issuers provide a replacement number on a separate document when consumers buy the cards. If the card is lost or stolen, the consumer can give the issuer the number to recover unused calling time.

The most common consumer problems with phone cards are:

- Access numbers or PINs that don't work;

- Card issuers who go out of business, leaving card-holders with a useless card;

- Customer service numbers that are busy or simply don't work;

- Access numbers that are constantly busy, preventing use of the card;

- Rates that are higher than advertised;

- Hidden connection charges, taxes and surcharges;

- Cards that expire without the consumer's knowledge;

- Cards that debit minutes even when the consumer doesn't connect with the party she's calling; and

- Poor quality connections.

Immigrants can avoid many of these problems by checking out a few things in advance:

1.   Ask if the retailer will stand behind the card if the telephone service is unsatisfactory.

2.   Look for the rate for domestic and international calls on the card's package or on the vending machine. These rates may vary depending on where you call. If you can't find the rate, call the card's customer service number.

3.  The pre-paid phone card industry is highly competitive. Beware of very low rates, particularly for international calls. They may indicate poor customer service.

4.  Look for disclosures about surcharges, monthly fees, per-call access, and the like, in addition to the rate-per-minute or unit. Some cards add a surcharge to the first minute of use. Others charge an activation fee for recharging cards.

5.  Check on expiration dates. Most cards expire one year after first use. If there is no expiration date, a card usually is considered "live" until all phone time is used.

6.  Look for a toll-free customer service number. If the customer service number isn't toll-free or displayed, it may be difficult to contact the company if you have a problem with the card. A busy signal on the customer service line may be a tip off to a rip-off.

7.  Be sure the card comes with instructions that you understand.

8.  Make sure the card comes in a sealed envelope or has a sticker covering the PIN. Otherwise, anyone who copies the PIN can use the phone time you've already paid for.

9.  Ask friends and relatives for references on the card you are thinking of buying. Or buy a small denomination first to test out the service.

**Phone Sharks.** Phone sharks are businesses that target low-income neighborhoods, selling pre-paid local telephone service. They "resell" local telephone service to consumers, encouraging them to believe that they have no other way of getting local phone service. Rates for these resellers are usually two to three times as high as the local telephone company, often for services that are not so complete or convenient. Phone sharks operate out of check-cashing outlets, rent-to-own stores, sometimes out of telephone companies, and often target immigrant communities.

Phone sharks typically charge hook-up fees (e.g., $40-$70) and high monthly charges (between $35 and $50 per month). The monthly charges are often two or three times as high as local telephone company flat rate charges for local service. The hook-up charges also tend to be higher.

Clients should be advised about the alternatives to phone sharks. An important alternative is Lifeline Assistance and Link-up programs. Lifeline telephone service is available to many income-eligible households in most states. In some states, qualifying households see as much as $13-14 off their local telephone bill each month. Most states also offer the "Link Up" program which reduces the hook-up (or connection) charges for qualifying low-income customers. More information about Lifeline and Link-up programs is available from your local telephone company, at www.lifelinesupport.org, and in the National Consumer Law Center's publication *Access to Utility Services* (2d ed. 2001).

## UTILITY ASSISTANCE PROGRAMS FOR LOW-INCOME FAMILIES

Stable utility service is critical to a family's survival. There are several ways for advocates to help immigrants who are having trouble with their utility bills. For example, there are a number of programs that can help clients pay for utility services and cut usage. These include:

**Level Payment Plans**. A level payment plan may help customers who are current on their utility bills, but who may have trouble paying their utility bills at certain times of the year, especially in the winter, when heating bills are high. To avoid running up debts during these months, customers can establish level payment plans with utility companies. In a level payment plan, a customer's projected yearly bill is divided into equal monthly installments; monthly bills reflect this amount rather than each month's actual costs. For example, a customer whose total gas bill for a year is $1200, would pay $100 each month instead of $200 to $300 a month in the winter, and $30 to $40 a month in the summer.

**Budget Payment Plans**. Households in financial distress can quickly get so far into the hole with their utility bills that a level payment plan is not enough. The household cannot catch up on back-due payments (called arrears) and also keep up current utility bills. One solution is for the consumer and utility to negotiate a budget payment plan whereby the consumer makes a fixed monthly payment and the utility promises not to shut off service.

To make a successful payment plan, the customer, preferably with the help of a counselor, must develop a simple budget that the household can reasonably meet, and must not be hesitant to push that plan with the utility company employee who negotiates the agreement. The utility company is likely to want a payment plan that requires larger payments than the customer can afford. Too many customers, believing they have no choice, agree to these payments.

Unrealistic plans, however, harm both customers and utility companies in the long run. The customer is unable to make the payments, and may lose the service, and the company does not collect its debt. In some states, utilities are not required to enter into a second payment plan with consumers who have defaulted on a first payment plan. If a company refuses to agree to a reasonable payment plan, help can be obtained from the consumer division of the local utility commission. Some utilities also are more willing to negotiate with consumer counselors than with consumers themselves.

**Federal Energy Assistance.** The federal Low Income Home Energy Assistance Program (LIHEAP), administered by the states, helps low-income households (families or individuals) pay their winter heating bills. Some states also use LIHEAP funds to assist with summer cooling expenses. All states set aside some of these funds to help out in times of crisis. LIHEAP benefits can also go to renters and even to some public and subsidized housing tenants, with the energy assistance payments usually going directly to the landlord's fuel supplier and the amount being credited against the family or individual's rent.

Guidelines for LIHEAP eligibility vary by state, but most states require that family income over the past three or twelve months be below 150% of the federal poverty guidelines. (In some states, income must be even less.) Under federal law, the household income for LIHEAP recipients cannot exceed 150 percent of the federal poverty guidelines or 60 percent of the state median income. The size of a household's LIHEAP benefits generally depends on its income and the number of household members, and may also depend on housing type, fuel type, fuel prices, weather conditions, or actual energy consumption.

To apply for LIHEAP benefits, the individual or family should contact the local agency in its community administering the program. This is usually a nonprofit agency, such as the local community action program (CAP), or a state welfare office. Benefits are usually paid directly to the utility company or fuel vendor, and the household's utility or fuel obligation is reduced accordingly.

**Utility Fuel Funds.** Many utility companies participate in special funds, sometimes directly subsidized by other customer contributions, to give loans or grants to those who cannot pay their utility bills. To determine the availability of these funds, contact the utility company or the local agency that administers the LIHEAP program.

**PIP, EAP and Other Special Payment Plans.** A growing number of utilities and state utility commissions are experimenting with plans by which individuals or families pay only a certain percentage of their income instead of the amount called for by their normal utility bills. Typically, if a low-income household regularly pays this lower payment schedule, it is rewarded by gradual forgiveness of its back bills, or arrears. These plans are sometimes called Percentage of Income Plans (PIPs) or Energy Assurance Plans (EAPs), but each utility seems to have its own unique name for the program. The best way to determine if a utility has such a program is to contact that particular utility or the public utility commission.

**Discounted Rates.** Some electric, gas and water utilities have special discounted rates for low-income, elderly and/or disabled households. Ask your utility company or the state public utilities commission about these discounted rates.

**Energy Conservation Programs.** Some states provide homeowners and tenants with funds to weatherize their homes, thereby reducing heating and cooling costs. Many utility companies provide low-cost loans or outright grants for home weatherization, and some have sizeable programs targeting low-income customers, providing weatherization services directly to customers.   More information on weatherization programs is usually available through local energy assistance offices.

Separate from such programs, individuals and families in many states can obtain assistance from utility companies to save on energy bills in other ways, such as replacing light bulbs with energy-efficient bulbs, insulating hot water tanks, and providing "low-flow" efficient faucets or shower heads. Again, many of these programs give special attention to low-income households.

**Other Government Programs.** Other state agencies, such as welfare departments, may also run small energy assistance programs. In particular, federally funded Emergency Assistance provides aid to households that within the past six months have had or currently have a member under age twenty-one.   Emergency Assistance can be provided only once in a twelve month period.   States may restrict the emergencies for which aid is provided, requiring, for example, that the emergency be unforeseen or out of the household's control.

**Charities and Other Private Sources.** Many charities, churches, and other private organizations help people pay their utility bills. These groups provide assistance only when they have funds available, and sometimes only at certain times of the year.

# HELPING AN IMMIGRANT FIGHT A TERMINATION OF SERVICE

The threat of immediate termination of service, and the need to restore service that has already been terminated, are the two most urgent problems faced by utility customers. In many states, statutes and public utility commission regulations provide a variety of significant protection against utility terminations. These protections include:

**Financial Hardship.** Public utility commission regulations in some states prohibit or restrict termination of service for households whose income falls below certain levels, or whose income is restricted to certain government benefits, or who can otherwise demonstrate financial hardship.

**Serious Illness.** Similarly, state law or public utility commission regulations often restrict termination of service for households whose members face a serious illness, are threatened with serious illness, or depend upon life support systems. Often, a doctor must certify the illness. A household with very young children may also be able to use the health risk to the children as grounds to stop utility termination.

**Winter Protection Rules.** Many states and cities have enacted legislation that prevents termination of utility service during certain times of the year, chiefly termination of heat-related services during the heating months. To qualify for the protection, financial hardship may have to be demonstrated.

**Tenant Protection.** It is all too common, particularly in difficult economic times, for a landlord to fail to pay for utility service, putting tenants at risk of losing the utility service. Tenants in this situation sometimes have special protection. In some states, tenants must receive a special shutoff notice if the landlord is delinquent (behind on his or her payment). Then, tenants make utility payments directly to the utility, and deduct those payments from their rent.

**Advance Notice of Utility Termination.** All customers are protected against surprise termination of service. Utility companies cannot legally terminate service without first providing customers with requests for payment and notices of termination. Many utilities must also provide customers with an opportunity to dispute or contest the reasons for the shutoff.

**Contesting the Termination.** A utility commission's consumer division responds to phone calls, letters, and visits by residential customers. Many of their complaints are resolved informally, by consultation between the consumer division and the utility. Consumer divisions also hold hearings on complaints that cannot be resolved informally. In large states, several hundred of these hearings are held each year. Consumers generally have a legal right to a hearing whenever they have grounds to dispute a utility termination. They must request the utility commission to provide a hearing before service is terminated. While municipal utilities are generally not regulated by the utility commission, customers of municipal utilities have a constitutional right to a hearing before termination. Consumers need not have a lawyer represent them at the hearing. However, it may be helpful to have an advocate assist with the hearing. To support their claim, it is important for consumers to bring all relevant documentary evidence, such as a physician's affidavit or past bills. It may also be helpful to have witnesses such as friends and neighbors present.

**Bankruptcy Protection.** The mere filing of a bankruptcy petition automatically requires the utility to restore service or cease a threatened termination. The bankruptcy filing creates a twenty-day period where the consumer has a right to service from all applicable utilities. The utility can only terminate service after that twenty-day period if the consumer fails to pay future bills, even if the consumer never pays another penny on past-due bills. The utility, though, can require that the consumer provide adequate assurance that future bills will be paid, such as the consumer providing a new deposit or requiring a co-signer to such an agreement.

# 13

# DEBT COLLECTION HARASSMENT

- *What Can a Debt Collector Really Do?*
- *How to Avoid Harassment*

Low-income clients trying to get their lives together, particularly those re-entering the work force or trying to rent an apartment or buy a home, often find that past debts continue to cause them problems. Particularly as immigrants attempt to prioritize debts and make the difficult choices about which debts to pay first, they are often lured into bad choices by collection agencies sending harassing letters and making phone calls.

This chapter contains a brief summary of important debt collection rights. In particular, clients should be counseled to avoid letting debt collectors pressure them into making the wrong choices about which debts to pay first.

## WHAT CAN A DEBT COLLECTOR REALLY DO?

A debt collector can do little more than demand payment. If the creditor has not taken the consumer's house, car, or other property as collateral on a loan, then legally the creditor can only do three things:

    1.   Stop doing business with the consumer.

2.  Report a default to a credit bureau (see Chapter 11, "Credit Reporting").

3.  Sue the consumer in court. (This threat may not be as serious as many consumers think. Many creditors do not follow through on their threats. Even if they do, consumers can raise defenses to paying the debt. And even if the creditor obtains a judgment, this judgment still does not force the consumer to pay the debt. It only gives the creditor the right to try to seize part of a consumer's wages or property.)

# HOW TO AVOID HARASSMENT

Federal law and many states prohibit harassment by collection agencies (and in some states by creditors). The federal law can be found at 15 U.S.C. § 1692 *et seq.* Most states also have fair debt laws. In many cases, the state laws provide additional protections. For example, the federal law applies only to third party collectors. Some state laws, in contrast, also cover creditors collecting their own debts. For more information about fair debt laws and other ways to challenge debt collector harassment, see NCLC's manual *Fair Debt Collection* (4th ed. 2000 and Supp.) This manual contains an appendix with a summary of state debt collection laws.

In general, consumers being harassed by debt collectors should follow these eight steps:

1.  Head off harassment before it starts

2.  Write a letter requesting the collector to stop collection efforts. This is often called a "cease communication" letter. Collectors must stop contacting the consumer after receiving this letter, with only a few limited exceptions. The collector can still sue the consumer. A sample "cease communication letter":

---

**SAMPLE LETTER**

---

[date]

[name of collection agency]
[address]

Name and
Account Number

Dear Agency:

 I am writing to request that you stop contacting me about account number _____ with [name of creditor] as required by the Fair Debt Collection Practices Act 15 U.S.C. section 1692c(c). (Note: Delete reference to the Act where the letter is to a creditor instead of to a collection agency. Some, but not all, state laws prohibit further contact by creditors.)

[Document any harassing contact by the collection agency. In some cases, provide information about why the consumer can't pay bill, or if appropriate, does not owe the money.]

This letter is not meant in any way to be an acknowledgment that I owe this money. I will take care of this matter when I can. Your cooperation will be appreciated.

[Signature]

---

3.  Have a lawyer write a cease communication letter.

4.  Work out a payment plan (make sure all essential debts have been taken care of first).

5.  Complain about billing errors.

6.  Complain to a government agency. Complaints about collector conduct should be sent to the Federal Trade Commission, Bureau of Consumer Protection, Washington, D.C. 20580, to the state consumer protection division, and to any local consumer protection office.

7.  File bankruptcy. Filing bankruptcy will instantly and effectively stop all debt collection efforts. Often simpler and less expensive action will resolve debt collection harassment, but bankruptcy filing may provide significant other advantages for the consumer.

8.  Sue the debt collector if appropriate.

# 14

# STUDENT LOANS

- *Types of Student Loans*
- *Federal Discharges*
- *Repayment Options*
- *Additional Resources*

Unfair and deceptive vocational and correspondence school practices are a tremendous source of frustration, financial loss, and loss of opportunity for consumers, particularly young, low-income consumers hoping to break out of poverty. The problem was particularly serious in the 1980s and early 1990s. Many of the trade school scams during this time were targeted at new immigrants. Trade schools sprang up in immigrant communities, many claiming to offer an English as a Second Language (ESL) component in addition to courses that would supposedly lead to good paying jobs as computer technicians, word processors, auto mechanics, and broadcasters.

Although many of the worst schools are now closed, former students continue to suffer the consequences due to defaulted loans for worthless educations that prevent them from returning to school and ruin their credit histories. In addition, new problems continue to surface. For-profit higher education is a booming market, increasingly dominated by regional and even national franchises, many with stock shares traded on Wall Street. There are already many complaints about some of these new "mega-schools." There is also room for abuse as more and more schools offer "distance education" similar to the former "correspondence schools" which allowed students to take courses by mail or computer.

Fortunately, many students can eliminate these debts or arrange payment plans that they can afford. A summary of these provisions is below. For more detail, see NCLC's publication *Student Loan Law* (2001).

# TYPES OF STUDENT LOANS

Depending on the type of discharge, the following loans can be discharged through some or all of the federal discharge programs:

- Guaranteed Student Loans (Stafford);

- Unsubsidized Stafford Loans;

- Supplemental Loans for Students (SLSs);

- PLUS Loans (Parent Borrowers);

- Federal Direct Loans;

- Perkins (no false certification discharges);

To find out more about what type of loan a client has, contact the National Student Loan Data System (NSLDS) through the Federal Student Aid Information Center, 1-800-4-FED-AID, TDD 1-800-730-8913 or on-line at www.nslds.ed.gov.

# FEDERAL DISCHARGES

These are the most powerful remedies available to student loan borrowers. The good news is that borrowers who qualify for discharges will have their loans cancelled and all money they have paid out or money that has been taken from them to pay the loans should be paid back. The government is also required to help remove negative information from credit reports related to the loans. The bad news is that not everyone qualifies for these discharges. Each federal discharge and the requirements to receive the discharges are summarized below.

**Closed School Discharge.**[1] Applies only to loans received at least in part on or after January 1, 1986. The student must have been enrolled at the time of school closure or if she withdrew, the withdrawal had to have occurred within 90 days of closure. The Department of Education maintains a list of official closure dates, available at:
http://www.ed.gov/offices/OSFAP/Students/closedschool/search.html.

Federal discharge forms can be downloaded from http://www.ed.gov/offices/OSFAP/DCS/forms/index.html.

**False Certification Discharge.**[2] Applies only to loans received at least in part on or after January 1, 1986. Perkins loans are not eligible.

To qualify, students must show that her eligibility to borrow was falsely certified by the school. In most cases, students with high school diplomas or G.E.D.s at the time of admission are not qualified. There are exceptions to the high school diploma requirement: A student may qualify if she was unable to meet minimum state employment requirements for the job for which the student was being trained, or if the school forged or altered the loan note or check endorsements. A copy of the false certification discharge form (abitily-to-benefit) is reprinted at Appendix 2.

**Unpaid Refund Discharge.**[3] A new discharge was passed as part of the 1998 Higher Education Act. This allows students to discharge loan liability for loans obtained after January 1, 1986 to the extent of the amount of a refund that a school owed the student and failed to pay.

**Disability Discharge.**[4] Borrowers can discharge loans if they can document a permanent and total disability. Pre-existing conditions qualify only if there has been deterioration. In 2002, the Department will begin implementing a conditional discharge program.

**Bankruptcy.** Currently the only ground for discharging a student loan in bankruptcy is if the student can show that repayment will "impose an undue hardship on the debtor and debtor's dependents."

There is no longer a discharge for loans more than seven years old. The elimination of the seven year discharge applies only to cases filed after October 7, 1998.

**State Discharges.** State tuition recovery funds (STRFs) can be a valuable source of relief for defrauded students where a school is insolvent and where the student cannot obtain a federal discharge. The majority of states have either a STRF or a bond program to reimburse defrauded students.[5]

# REPAYMENT OPTIONS

There are many special repayment options for student loan borrowers. These plans are particularly effective for borrowers who do not qualify for federal or state discharges. In addition, deferments may be available for those not already in default. The primary types of deferments are: student (or in-school) deferments, unemployment deferments not to exceed three years, and economic hardship deferments, granted one year at a time for a maximum of three years.

Forbearances are available even when a borrower is in default. These are less advantageous than deferments because interest continues to accrue while the loan payments are reduced or postponed.

Loan consolidation is another possibility, particularly for those who do not qualify for discharges, but wish to get new loans and grants. Borrowers can consolidate their defaulted student loans into a Federal Direct Consolidation Loan with an Income Contingent Repayment Plan (ICRP). Applications can be obtained by calling 1-800-557-7392 or on-line at http://www.ed.gov/directloan. A copy of an application form is reprinted at Appendix 2.

An on-line calculator can be used to figure out the monthly payment under standard and income contingent repayment plans. See http://www.ed.gov/DirectLoan/Repay/Calc/dlentry2.html.

Another option is for borrowers to request a reasonable and affordable payment plan based on their total financial circumstances or to try to rehabilitate their loans.

# ADDITIONAL RESOURCES

The National Consumer Law Center publishes a manual, *Student Loan Law: Collections, Intercepts, Deferments, Discharges, Repayment Plans, and Trade School Abuses* (2001). For information, please call NCLC publications at 617-523-8089.

The Department of Education has an ombudsman office that will assist student loan borrowers. The toll-free phone number is 877-557-2575; www.sfahelp.ed.gov. Borrowers should first try to work out problems on their own before contacting the ombudsman office.

The Department of Education has a helpful web site: www.ed.gov. The Department's "Student Guide" is available in English and Spanish on the web site or by calling the Federal Student Aid Information Center at 1-800-4-FED-AID.

---

[1] 34 C.F.R. §682.402(d).

[2] 34 C.F.R. §682.402(e).

[3] 34 C.F.R. §682.402(l).

[4] 34 C.F.R. § 682.402(c).

[5] For more information on STRFs, see Student Loan Manual §9.6.1.

# 15

# CREDIT DISCRIMINATION

Credit discrimination permeates American society. Minorities and other protected groups face difficulties obtaining market-rate first and second mortgages. Many banks do not even open branches in minority neighborhoods. Creditors discriminate as to which customers they solicit for credit, to whom they grant credit, or how their credit customers are treated in subsequent stages of the credit transaction, such as in loan servicing and debt collection. Many consumers are not even sure if they are eligible for credit or do not understand why they are turned down for credit.

Discrimination cuts off access to credit for the neediest consumers. Even though a common perception is that low-income people do not need credit and that they cannot afford it, the reality is that the need to establish credit is so pervasive that it affects many aspects of ordinary existence. For example, the absence of credit or "bad" credit may be why a client is denied admission to rental housing or prevented from opening a bank account.

There is a direct and measurable cost of this discrimination. Predatory, high-interest rate, first and second mortgage lenders and others target the very groups discriminated against by traditional lenders. Another direct consequence of credit discrimination is lost opportunity for home ownership, lost opportunity for a college education, and denial of access to medical care and other essential services.

The key federal laws prohibiting credit discrimination are:

- The Equal Credit Opportunity Act (ECOA);[1]

- The Fair Housing Act (FHA);[2]

- Other federal civil rights acts such as 42 U.S.C. §§ 1981 and 1982;

- State credit discrimination laws[3].

Many of these laws can be used to protect immigrants who are discriminated against either on the basis of national origin or race. For example, national origin is a prohibited basis under the ECOA, and in certain aspects under the federal civil rights acts. "National origin" means a persons' ancestry. Denying credit because a person does not speak English should also be a form of discrimination based on national origin. Creditors, may, however inquire about and consider an applicant's permanent residence and immigration status.

In many cases, the immigrant may not be facing discrimination due to national origin, but rather due to race, age, gender, or another prohibited basis. The laws listed above are critical tools in fighting discrimination on all of these bases. To get a better understanding of which laws apply to which types of discrimination, see NCLC's manual *Credit Discrimination* (2d ed. 1998 and Supp.).

Additional information is available on the following government web sites:

- Department of Housing and Urban Development (http://www.hud.gov);

- Federal Trade Commission (http://www.ftc.gov);

- Federal Reserve Board (http://www.federalreserve.gov).

---

[1]  15 U.S.C. §§ 1691-1691f; Reg. B, 12 C.F.R. § 202.

[2]  42 U.S.C. § 3601 - 3631

[3]  For more information, see National Consumer Law Center, Credit Discrimination (2d ed. 1998 & Supp.).

— Appendix 1—

# Budget Charts

| INCOME BUDGET | | | | |
|---|---|---|---|---|
| SOURCE OF INCOME | LAST MONTH ACTUAL (1) | THIS MONTH EXPECTED (2) | THIS MONTH ACTUAL (3) | ADJUSTED MONTHLY (4) |
| Employment (5) | $ | $ | $ | $ |
| Overtime | | | | |
| Child Support/Alimony (7) | | | | |
| Pension | | | | |
| Interest | | | | |
| Public Benefits (8) | | | | |
| Dividends | | | | |
| Trust Payments | | | | |
| Royalties | | | | |
| Rents Received | | | | |
| Other (List) (9) | | | | |
| | | | | |
| | | | | |
| | | | | |
| | | | | |
| TOTAL (MONTHLY) | $ | $ | $ | $ |

# NOTES

**(1)** This should be based on your income records for the past month.

**(2)** This column should include your best projections of your regular monthly income for coming months.

**(3)** After making your initial budget, keep careful records for the next month. Then fill in your actual income from each source. This will help you determine if your actual income meets your budget projections.

**(4)** After keeping records of your actual income for at least a month, go back and fill in this column based on your experience. Although this column will be a projection for the future, it should be more accurate than the projection you made when you started the budgeting process, because it will be based on actual monthly income for one month or more.

**(5)** Include the income of all household members who will be contributing to the family budget.

**(6)** You can list either your take home pay or your total employment income. If you use the total, remember to list all of your payroll deductions as expenses in the expense budget. If you use your take home pay, remember to check your pay stub to make sure that there are no unnecessary deductions.

**(7)** Include only the amounts you are actually expecting to receive, if any.

**(8)** This should include all money received from public benefits each month including food stamps, welfare, social security, disability, unemployment compensation, worker's compensation etc. If you are receiving more than one type of income, then you may want to use as box labeled "other" at the bottom of the budget.

**(9)** If you need more space, combine two or more other sources of income on a separate sheet and then list them together as one line in your budget.

**(10)** Include the total expenses of everyone in your household who shares expenses.

**(11)** This should be based, as closely as possible, on your experience in the most recent month. Estimate items for which you have not kept complete records.

**(12)** This column should include your best projections of your monthly expenses for coming months.

**(13)** After making your initial budget, keep careful records for the next month. Then fill in your actual expenses for each item. This will help you determine if your actual expenses meet the budgeted amount.

**(14)** After keeping records of your actual expenses for at least a month, go back and fill in this column based on your experience. Although this column will be a projection for the future, it should be more accurate than the projection you made when you started the budgeting process, because it will be based on actual monthly expenses for one month or more.

**(15)** Do *not* fill this section out if you have used your take home pay in your income budget. However, you should check your pay stub to make sure that there are no unnecessary deductions from your pay. *Do fill this section out if you used your gross employment income budget or if you are self employed.*

**(16)** Bankruptcy can eliminate many types of wage garnishments. See NCLC's *Surviving Debt* Chapter Twenty (3rd. ed. 1999).

**(17)** These payments can usually be eliminated during a period of financial hardship.

**(18)** Ways to keep your home during periods of financial crisis are discussed in NCLC's *Surviving Debt* Chapters Eleven through Fourteen (3rd. ed. 1999) if you own, and in Chapter Fifteen if you are a renter.

| EXPENSE BUDGET | | | | |
|---|---|---|---|---|
| TYPE OF EXPENSE (10) | LAST MONTH ACTUAL (11) | THIS MONTH EXPECTED (12) | THIS MONTH ACTUAL (13) | ADJUSTED MONTH (14) |
| Payroll Deduction (15) | | | | |
| Income Tax Withheld | | | | |
| Social Security | | | | |
| FICA | | | | |
| Wage Garnishments (16) | | | | |
| Credit Union (17) | | | | |
| Other | | | | |
| Home Related Expenses (18) | | | | |
| Mortgage or Rent (19) | | | | |
| Second Mortgage | | | | |
| Third Mortgage | | | | |
| Real Estate Taxes (20) | | | | |
| Insurance (21) | | | | |
| Condo Fees & | | | | |
| Mobile Home Lot Rent | | | | |
| Home Maintenance/Upkeep | | | | |
| Utilities (22) | | | | |
| Gas | | | | |
| Electric | | | | |
| Oil | | | | |
| Water/Sewer | | | | |
| Telephone | | | | |
| Other (23) | | | | |
| Food | | | | |
| Clothing | | | | |
| Laundry and Cleaning | | | | |
| Medical (24) | | | | |
| Current Needs | | | | |
| Prescriptions | | | | |
| Dental | | | | |
| Other | | | | |
| SUBTOTAL PAGE 1 | | | | |

| | | | | |
|---|---|---|---|---|
| **Transportation** | | | | |
|   Auto Payments | | | | |
|   Car Insurance | | | | |
|   Gas and Maintenance | | | | |
|   Public Transportation | | | | |
| Life Insurance | | | | |
| Alimony or Support Paid | | | | |
| Student Loan Payments (25) | | | | |
| Amounts Owed on Debts (26) | | | | |
|   Credit Card (27) | | | | |
|   Credit Card | | | | |
|   Credit Card | | | | |
|   Medical Bill (28) | | | | |
|   Medical Bill | | | | |
| Other Back Bills (List)(29) | | | | |
| | | | | |
| | | | | |
| Cosigned Debts (30) | | | | |
| Business Debts (List)(31) | | | | |
| | | | | |
| | | | | |
| | | | | |
| Other Expenses (List)(32) | | | | |
| | | | | |
| | | | | |
| | | | | |
| Miscellaneous (33) | | | | |
| **TOTAL** | | | | |

| INCOME AND EXPENSE TOTALS | | | | |
|---|---|---|---|---|
| | LAST MONTH ACTUAL | THIS MONTH EXPECTED | THIS MONTH ACTUAL | ADJUSTED EXPECTED |
| A. TOTAL PROJECTED MONTHLY INCOME (34) | | | | |
| B. TOTAL PROJECTED MONTHLY EXPENSES (35) | | | | |
| EXCESS INCOME OR SHORTFALL (A MINUS B) | | | | |

## NOTES

**(19)** Include amounts here only for your primary home. If you have a vacation home or a time share, include that separately below under "other expenses". This will help you determine whether you can make ends meet by giving up your second home or time share.

**(20)** Include your real estate taxes only if these amounts are not included with your escrow payment on your mortgage.

**(21)** Include your home insurance payments if these amounts are for renter's insurance or if they are not included with your escrow payment on your mortgage.

**(22)** Many options for reducing these amounts are discussed in NCLC's *Surviving Debt* Chapter Fourteen (3rd. ed. 1999).

**(23)** For example, propane and cable television subscriptions are discussed in NCLC's *Surviving Debt* Chapter Sixteen (3rd. ed. 1999).

**(24)** This should not include your back bills. Back medical bills are unsecured debts which should be handled differently in your budget and listed below under "Amounts Owed on Debts". Generally, they should only be paid in times of financial hardship if you can afford to pay. Strategies for dealing with back medical bills and other unsecured debts are covered in NCLC's *Surviving Debt* Chapter One (3rd. ed. 1999).

**(25)** Many options for dealing with or reducing student loan obligations are discussed in NCLC's *Surviving Debt* Chapter Nineteen (3rd. ed. 1999).

**(26)** List here the monthly payments you plan to make on your unsecured debts like credit cards and medical bills. These are low priority debts as discussed in NCLC's *Surviving Debt* Chapter One (3rd. ed. 1999). You may plan to pay little or nothing if you are trying to deal with other more important expenses on a limited income. It does not make sense to make even "minimum" payments on these debts unless you can afford to do so after paying for your necessities and higher priority bills. A variety of choices for dealing with these debts and with collection activities by creditors are discussed in *Surviving Debt* Chapters One and Six. Dealing with lawsuits on unsecured debts is discussed in *Surviving Debt* Chapter Eight. Using bankruptcy to address unsecured debts is discussed in *Surviving Debt* Chapter Twenty.

**(27)** In most cases you should list the minimum required payment unless you can afford to pay more. This can be costly however, since with credit card bills, interest will mount up very quickly if you pay only the minimum. If you cannot afford even the minimum monthly payment, then list zero and look into your other options for dealing with these debts as discussed in the prior note.

**(28)** List your back bills here. Current anticipated medical expenses should be listed separately above as a higher priority expense. Old bills can generally be dealt with like other low priority unsecured debts.

**(29)** Some examples might include other debts owed to professionals such as lawyers or accountants, personal loans, bills owed to prior landlords, deficiency claims on prior foreclosures or repossessions and any other debt for which the creditor has no collateral.

**(30)** You need to treat debts on which you are a cosigner as a high priority debt if you have given your property as collateral for the debt. Cosigned debts are a lower priority if your property does not serve as collateral. See NCLC's *Surviving Debt* Chapter One (3rd. ed. 1999).

**(31)** Your obligations on business related debts can be complicated and depends on the type of business. You may want to get special legal assistance on whether payment on these debts should be included in your budget as a high priority.

**(32)** Everyone has a different situation. You should think about any other source of regular household expenses and list them here. Some frequently overlooked items include cigarettes, diapers, pet related expenses, children's allowances, lay-away payments, rent-to-own, etc. Some of these items can be quite costly and will throw your budget out of whack if they are not accounted for.

**(33)** You may want to include a small sum here for the miscellaneous small expenses or for emergencies which are unaccounted for elsewhere.

**(34)** Take this amount from your income budget above.

**(35)** Take this amount from your expense budget above.

**(36)** If you have excess income — congratulations. However, make sure that your budget actually works by trying it out for a few months. You may want to use your excess income to pay down any back debts which are carrying interest — particularly credit cards. If you have a shortfall, you should consider limiting or ending any discretionary items in your budget, terminating payment on your credit cards in order to maintain your necessities and reading the rest of this book for strategies to use to help you survive your debt while you are getting back on your feet.

# -- Appendix 2 --

# AFFIDAVIT OF SUPPORT

The affidavit of support form contained in this appendix is a sample form only. Copies suitable for filing with INS are available on the INS web site at www.ins.usdoj.gov. Forms may also be obtained directly from local INS offices.

OMB No. 1115-0214

**U.S. Department of Justice**
Immigration and Naturalization Service

# Affidavit of Support Under Section 213A of the Act

## INSTRUCTIONS

### Purpose of this Form
This form is required to show that an intending immigrant has adequate means of financial support and is not likely to become a public charge.

### Sponsor's Obligation
The person completing this affidavit is the sponsor. A sponsor's obligation continues until the sponsored immigrant becomes a U.S. citizen, can be credited with 40 qualifying quarters of work, departs the United States permanently, or dies. Divorce does not terminate the obligation. By executing this form, you, the sponsor, agree to support the intending immigrant and any spouse and/or children immigrating with him or her and to reimburse any government agency or private entity that provides these sponsored immigrants with Federal, State, or local means-tested public benefits.

### General Filing Instructions
Please answer all questions by typing or clearly printing in black ink only. Indicate that an item is not applicable with "N/A". If an answer is "none," please so state. If you need extra space to answer any item, attach a sheet of paper with your name and Social Security number, and indicate the number of the item to which the answer refers.

You must submit an affidavit of support for each applicant for immigrant status. You may submit photocopies of this affidavit for any spouse or children immigrating with an immigrant you are sponsoring. For purposes of this form, a spouse or child is immigrating with an immigrant you are sponsoring if he or she is:   1) listed in Part 3 of this affidavit of support; and 2) applies for an immigrant visa or adjustment of status within 6 months of the date this affidavit of support is originally completed and signed. The signature on the affidavit must be notarized by a notary public or signed before an Immigration or a Consular officer.

You should give the completed affidavit of support with all required documentation to the sponsored immigrant for submission to either a Consular Officer with Form OF-230, Application for Immigrant Visa and Alien Registration, or an Immigration Officer with Form I-485, Application to Register Permanent Residence or Adjust Status. You may enclose the affidavit of support and accompanying documents in a sealed envelope to be opened only by the designated Government official. The sponsored immigrant must submit the affidavit of support to the Government within 6 months of its signature.

### Who Needs an Affidavit of Support under Section 213A?
This affidavit must be filed at the time an intending immigrant is applying for an immigrant visa or adjustment of status. It is required for:

- All immediate relatives, including orphans, and family-based immigrants. (Self-petitioning widow/ers and battered spouses and children are exempt from this requirement); and

- Employment-based immigrants where a relative filed the immigrant visa petition or has a significant ownership interest (5 percent or more) in the entity that filed the petition.

### Who Completes an Affidavit of Support under Section 213A?
- For immediate relatives and family-based immigrants, the family member petitioning for the intending immigrant must be the sponsor.

- For employment-based immigrants, the petitioning relative or a relative with a significant ownership interest (5 percent or more) in the petitioning entity must be the sponsor. The term "relative," for these purposes, is defined as husband, wife, father, mother, child, adult son or daughter, brother, or sister.

- If the petitioner cannot meet the income requirements, a joint sponsor may submit an additonal affidavit of support.

A sponsor, or joint sponsor, must also be:

- A citizen or national of the United States or an alien lawfully admitted to the United States for permanent residence;

- At least 18 years of age; and

- Domiciled in the United States or its territories and possessions.

### Sponsor's Income Requirement
As a sponsor, your household income must equal or exceed 125 percent of the Federal poverty line for your household size.  For the purpose of the affidavit of support, household size includes yourself, all persons related to you by birth, marriage, or adoption living in your residence, your dependents, any immigrants you have previously sponsored using INS Form I-864 if that obligation has not terminated, and the intending immigrant(s) in Part 3 of this affidavit of support. The poverty guidelines are calculated and published annually by the Department of Health and Human Services. Sponsors who are on active duty in the U.S. Armed Forces other than for training need only demonstrate income at 100 percent of the poverty line *if* they are submitting this affidavit for the purpose of sponsoring their spouse or child.

If you are currently employed and have an *individual* income which meets or exceeds 125 percent of the Federal poverty line (100 percent, if applicable) for your household size, you do not need to list the income of any other person. When determining your income, you may include the income generated by individuals related to you by birth, marriage, or adoption who are living in your residence, if they have lived in your residence for the previous 6 months, or who are listed as dependents on your most recent Federal income tax return whether or not they live in your residence. For their income to be considered, these household members or dependents must be willing to make their income available for the support of the sponsored immigrant(s) if necessary, and to complete and sign Form I-864A, Contract Between Sponsor and Household Member. However, a household member who is the immigrant you are sponsoring only need complete Form I-864A if his or her income will be used to determine your ability to support a spouse and/or children immigrating with him or her.

If in any of the most recent 3 tax years, you and your spouse each reported income on a joint income tax return, but you want to use only your own income to qualify (and your spouse is not submitting a Form I-864A), you may provide a separate breakout of your individual income for these years. Your individual income will be based on the earnings from your W-2 forms, Wage and Tax Statement, submitted to IRS for any such years. If necessary to meet the income requirement, you may also submit evidence of other income listed on your tax returns which can be attributed to you. You must provide documentation of such reported income, including Forms 1099 sent by the payer, which show your name and Social Security number.

You must calculate your household size and total household income as indicated in Parts 4.C. and 4.D. of this form. You must compare your total household income with the minimum income requirement for your household size using the poverty guidelines. For the purposes of the affidavit of support, determination of your ability to meet the income requirements will be based on the most recent poverty guidelines published in the Federal Register at the time the Consular or Immigration Officer makes a decision on the intending immigrant's application for an immigrant visa or adjustment of status. Immigration and Consular Officers will begin to use updated poverty guidelines on the first day of the second month after the date the guidelines are published in the Federal Register.

If your total household income is equal to or higher than the minimum income requirement for your household size, you do not need to provide information on your assets, and you may *not* have a joint sponsor unless you are requested to do so by a Consular or Immigration Officer. If your total household income does not meet the minimum income requirement, the intending immigrant will be ineligible for an immigrant visa or adjustment of status, unless:

- You provide evidence of assets that meet the requirements outlined under "Evidence of Assets" below; and/or

- The immigrant you are sponsoring provides evidence of assets that meet the requirements under "Evidence of Assets" below; or

- A joint sponsor assumes the liability of the intending immigrant with you. A joint sponsor must execute a separate affidavit of support on behalf of the intending

immigrant and any accompanying family members. A joint sponsor must individually meet the minimum requirement of 125 percent of the poverty line based on his or her household size and income and/or assets, including any assets of the sponsored immigrant.

The Government may pursue verification of any information provided on or in support of this form, including employment, income, or assets with the employer, financial or other institutions, the Internal Revenue Service, or the Social Security Administration.

### Evidence of Income
In order to complete this form you must submit the following evidence of income:

- A copy of your complete Federal income tax return, as filed with the Internal Revenue Service, for each of the most recent 3 tax years. If you were not required to file a tax return in any of the most recent 3 tax years, you must provide an explanation. If you filed a joint income tax return and are using only your own income to qualify, you must also submit copies of your W-2s for each of the most recent 3 tax years, and if necessary to meet the income requirement, evidence of other income reported on your tax returns, such as Forms 1099.

- If you rely on income of any members of your household or dependents in order to reach the minimum income requirement, copies of their Federal income tax returns for the most recent 3 tax years. These persons must each complete and sign a Form I-864A, Contract Between Sponsor and Household Member.

- Evidence of current employment or self-employment, such as a recent pay statement, or a statement from your employer on business stationery, showing beginning date of employment, type of work performed, and salary or wages paid. You must also provide evidence of current employment for any person whose income is used to qualify.

### Evidence of Assets
If you want to use your assets, the assets of your household members or dependents, and/or the assets of the immigrant you are sponsoring to meet the minimum income requirement, you must provide evidence of assets with a cash value that equals at least five times the difference between your total household income and the minimum income requirement. For the assets of a household member, other than the immigrant(s) you are sponsoring, to be considered, the household member must complete and sign Form I-864A, Contract Between Sponsor and Household Member.

All assets must be supported with evidence to verify location, ownership, and value of each asset. Any liens and liabilities relating to the assets must be documented. List only assets that can be readily converted into cash within one year. Evidence of assets includes, but is not limited to the following:

- Bank statements covering the last 12 months, *or a* statement from an officer of the bank or other financial institution in which you have deposits, including deposit/withdrawal history for the last 12 months, and current balance;
- Evidence of ownership and value of stocks, bonds, and certificates of deposit, and date(s) acquired;
- Evidence of ownership and value of other personal property, and date(s) acquired; and
- Evidence of ownership and value of any real estate, and date(s) acquired.

### Change of Sponsor's Address

You are required by 8 U.S.C. 1183a(d) and 8 CFR 213a.3 to report every change of address to the Immigration and Naturalization Service and the State(s) in which the sponsored immigrant(s) reside(s). You must report changes of address to INS on Form I-865, Sponsor's Notice of Change of Address, within 30 days of any change of address. You must also report any change in your address to the State(s) in which the sponsored immigrant(s) live.

### Penalties

If you include in this affidavit of support any material information that you know to be false, you may be liable for criminal prosecution under the laws of the United States.

If you fail to give notice of your change of address, as required by 8 U.S.C. 1183a(d) and 8 CFR 213a.3, you may be liable for the civil penalty established by 8 U.S.C. 1183a(d)(2). The amount of the civil penalty will depend on whether you failed to give this notice because you were aware that the inimigrant(s) you sponsored had received Federal, State, or local means-tested public benefits.

### Privacy Act Notice

Authority for the collection of the information requested on this form is contained in 8 U.S.C. 1182(a)(4), 1183a, 1184(a), and 1258. The information will be used principally by the INS or by any Consular Officer to whom it is furnished, to support an alien's application for benefits under the Immigration and Nationality Act and specifically the assertion that he or she has adequate means of financial support and will not become a public charge. Submission of the information is voluntary. Failure to provide the information will result in denial of the application for an immigrant visa or adjustment of status.

The information may also, as a matter of routine use, be disclosed to other Federal, State, and local agencies or private entities providing means-tested public benefits for use in civil action against the sponsor for breach of contract. It may also be disclosed as a matter of routine use to other Federal, State, local, and foreign law enforcement and regulatory agencies to enable these entities to carry out their law enforcement responsibilites.

### Reporting Burden

A person is not required to respond to a collection of information unless it displays a currently valid OMB control number. We try to create forms and instructions that are accurate, can be easily understood, and which impose the least possible burden on you to provide us with information. Often this is difficult because some immigration laws are very complex. The reporting burden for this collection of information on Form I-864 is computed as follows: 1) learning about the form, 17 minutes; 2) completing the form, 22 minutes; and 3) assembling and filing the form, 30 minutes, for an estimated average of 69 minutes per response. The reporting burden for collection of information on Form I-864A is computed as: 1) learning about the form, 5 minutes; 2) completing the form, 8 minutes; 3) assembling and filing the form, 2 minutes, for an estimated average of 15 minutes per response. If you have comments regarding the accuracy of this estimates, or suggestions for making this form simpler, you can write to the Immigration and Naturalization Service, HQPDI, 425 I Street, N.W., Room 4034, Washington, DC 20536. **DO NOT MAIL YOUR COMPLETED AFFIDAVIT OF SUPPORT TO THIS ADDRESS.**

### CHECK LIST

**The following items must be submitted with Form I-864, Affidavit of Support Under Section 213A:**

**For *ALL* sponsors:**

☐ This form, the **I-864, completed and signed** before a notary public or a Consular or Immigration Officer.

☐ Proof of **current employment** or self employment.

☐ Your individual Federal **income tax returns for the most recent 3 tax years**, or an explanation if fewer are submitted. Your **W-2s** for any of the most recent 3 tax years for which you filed a joint tax return but are using only your own income to qualify. Forms 1099 or evidence of other reported income *if* necessary to qualify.

**For *SOME* sponsors:**

☐ *If the immigrant you are sponsoring is bringing a spouse or children,* **photocopies of the immigrant's affidavit of support** for each spouse and/or child immigrating with the immigrant you are sponsoring.

☐ *If you are on active duty in the U.S. Armed Forces and are sponsoring a spouse or child using the 100 percent of poverty level exception,* **proof of your active military status.**

*If you are using the income of persons in your household or dependents to qualify,*

☐ A separate **Form I-864A** for each person whose income you will use. A sponsored immigrant/household member who is not immigrating with a spouse and/or child **does not need to complete Form I-864A.**

☐ Proof of their **residency and relationship** to you if they are not listed as dependents on your income tax return for the most recent tax year.

☐ Proof of their **current employment** or self-employment.

☐ Copies of their individual Federal **income tax returns for the 3 most recent tax years,** or an explanation if fewer are submitted.

*If you use your assets or the assets of the sponsored immigrant to qualify,*

☐ **Documentation of assets** establishing location, ownership, date of acquisition, and value. Evidence of any liens or liabilities against these assets.

☐ A separate **Form I-864A** for each household member other than the sponsored immigrant/household member.

*If you or a household member or dependent has used any type of means-tested public benefits in the last 3 years,*

☐ **A list of the programs and dates.**

*If you are a joint sponsor or the relative of an employment-based immigrant requiring an affidavit of support,* **proof of your citizenship status.**

☐ For U.S. citizens or nationals, a copy of your birth certificate, passport, or certificate of naturalization or citizenship.

☐ For lawful permanent residents, a copy of both sides of your I-551, Permanent Resident Card.

OMB No. 1115-0214

**U.S. Department of Justice**
Immigration and Naturalization Service

## Affidavit of Support Under Section 213A of the Act

**START HERE - Please Type or Print**

## Part 1. Information on Sponsor (You)

| Last Name | First Name | Middle Name |
|---|---|---|

| Mailing Address *(Street Number and Name)* | Apt/Suite Number |
|---|---|

| City | State or Province |
|---|---|

| Country | ZIP/Postal Code | Telephone Number |
|---|---|---|

| Place of Residence if different from above *(Street Number and Name)* | Apt/Suite Number |
|---|---|

| City | State or Province |
|---|---|

| Country | ZIP/Postal Code | Telephone Number |
|---|---|---|

| Date of Birth *(Month, Day, Year)* | Place of Birth *(City, State, Country)* | Are you a U.S. Citizen? ☐ Yes ☐ No |
|---|---|---|

| Social Security Number | A-Number *(If any)* |
|---|---|

**FOR AGENCY USE ONLY**

| This Affidavit | Receipt |
|---|---|
| [ ] Meets | |
| [ ] Does not meet | |
| Requirements of Section 213A | |

## Part 2. Basis for Filing Affidavit of Support

I am filing this affidavit of support because *(check one)*:

a. ☐  I filed/am filing the alien relative petition.

b. ☐  I filed/am filing an alien worker petition on behalf of the intending immigrant, who is related to me as my _____ .
*(relationship)*

c. ☐  I have ownership interest of at least 5% of _____ .
*(name of entity which filed visa petition)*
which filed an alien worker petition on behalf of the intending immigrant, who is related to me as my _____ .
*(relationship)*

d. ☐  I am a joint sponsor willing to accept the legal obligations with any other sponsor(s).

Officer or I.J. Signature

Location

Date

## Part 3. Information on the Immigrant(s) You Are Sponsoring

| Last Name | First Name | Middle Name |
|---|---|---|

| Date of Birth *(Month,Day, Year)* | Sex ☐ Male ☐ Female | Social Security Number *(If any)* |
|---|---|---|

| Country of Citizenship | A-Number *(If any)* |
|---|---|

| Current Address *(Street Number and Name)* | Apt/Suite Number | City |
|---|---|---|

| State/Province | Country | ZIP/Postal Code | Telephone Number |
|---|---|---|---|

List any spouse and/or children immigrating with the immigrant named above in this Part: *(Use additional sheet of paper if necessary.)*

| Name | Relationship to Sponsored Immigrant | | | Date of Birth | | | A-Number *(If any)* | Social Security Number *(If any)* |
|---|---|---|---|---|---|---|---|---|
| | Spouse | Son | Daughter | Mo. | Day | Yr. | | |
| | | | | | | | | |
| | | | | | | | | |
| | | | | | | | | |
| | | | | | | | | |

Form I-864 (09/26/00)Y

## Part 4. Eligibility to Sponsor

To be a sponsor you must be a U.S. citizen or national or a lawful permanent resident. If you are not the petitioning relative, you must provide proof of status. To prove status, U.S. citizens or nationals must attach a copy of a document proving status, such as a U.S. passport, birth certificate, or certificate of naturalization, and lawful permanent residents must attach a copy of both sides of their Permanent Resident Card (Form I-551).

The determination of your eligibility to sponsor an immigrant will be based on an evaluation of your demonstrated ability to maintain an annual income at or above 125 percent of the Federal poverty line (100 percent if you are a petitioner sponsoring your spouse or child and you are on active duty in the U.S. Armed Forces). The assessment of your ability to maintain an adequate income will include your current employment, household size, and household income as shown on the Federal income tax returns for the 3 most recent tax years. Assets that are readily converted to cash and that can be made available for the support of sponsored immigrants if necessary, including any such assets of the immigrant(s) you are sponsoring, may also be considered.

The greatest weight in determining eligibility will be placed on current employment and household income. If a petitioner is unable to demonstrate ability to meet the stated income and asset requirements, a joint sponsor who *can* meet the income and asset requirements is needed. Failure to provide adequate evidence of income and/or assets or an affidavit of support completed by a joint sponsor will result in denial of the immigrant's application for an immigrant visa or adjustment to permanent resident status.

### A. Sponsor's Employment

I am:  1. ☐ Employed by _____ *(Provide evidence of employment)*

           Annual salary $ _____ or hourly wage $ _____ *(for* _____ *hours per week)*

      2. ☐ Self employed _____ *(Name of business)*

           Nature of employment or business _____

      3. ☐ Unemployed or retired since _____

### B. Use of Benefits

Have you or anyone related to you by birth, marriage, or adoption living in your household or listed as a dependent on your most recent income tax return received any type of means-tested public benefit in the past 3 years?

☐ Yes   ☐ No *(If yes, provide details, including programs and dates, on a separate sheet of paper)*

### C. Sponsor's Household Size

                                           **Number**

1. Number of persons (related to you by birth, marriage, or adoption) living in your residence, including yourself *(Do NOT include persons being sponsored in this affidavit.)* _____

2. Number of immigrants being sponsored in this affidavit *(Include all persons in Part 3.)* _____

3. Number of immigrants **NOT** living in your household whom you are obligated to support under a previously signed Form I-864. _____

4. Number of persons who are otherwise dependent on you, as claimed in your tax return for the most recent tax year. _____

5. Total household size. *(Add lines 1 through 4.)*      **Total** _____ 0

List persons below who are included in lines 1 or 3 for whom you previously have submitted INS Form I-864, *if your support obligation has not terminated.*

*(If additional space is needed, use additional paper)*

| Name | A-Number | Date Affidavit of Support Signed | Relationship |
|---|---|---|---|
|  |  |  |  |
|  |  |  |  |
|  |  |  |  |
|  |  |  |  |
|  |  |  |  |
|  |  |  |  |

**Part 4.    Eligibility to Sponsor** *(Continued)*

## D. Sponsor's Annual Household Income

Enter total unadjusted income from your Federal income tax return for the most recent tax year below. If you last filed a joint income tax return but are using only your *own* income to qualify, list total earnings from your W-2 Forms, or, *if* necessary to reach the required income for your household size, include income from other sources listed on your tax return. If your *individual* income does not meet the income requirement for your household size, you may also list total income for anyone related to you by birth, marriage, or adoption currently living with you in your residence if they have lived in your residence for the previous 6 months, or any person shown as a dependent on your Federal income tax return for the most recent tax year, even if not living in the household. For their income to be considered, household members or dependents must be willing to make their income available for support of the sponsored immigrant(s) and to complete and sign Form I-864A, Contract Between Sponsor and Household Member. A sponsored immigrant/household member only need complete Form I-864A if his or her income will be used to determine your ability to support a spouse and/or children immigrating with him or her.

*You must attach evidence of current employment and copies of income tax returns as filed with the IRS for the most recent 3 tax years for yourself and all persons whose income is listed below. See "Required Evidence " in Instructions.* Income from all 3 years will be considered in determining your ability to support the immigrant(s) you are sponsoring.

☐ I filed a single/separate tax return for the most recent tax year.
☐ I filed a joint return for the most recent tax year which includes only my own income.
☐ I filed a joint return for the most recent tax year which includes income for my spouse and myself.
  ☐ I am submitting documentation of my individual income (Forms W-2 and 1099).
  ☐ I am qualifying using my spouse's income; my spouse is submitting a Form I-864A.

**Indicate most recent tax year**                                    _____
                                                                     *(tax year)*

Sponsor's individual income                                    $ _____

**or**

Sponsor and spouse's combined income                           $ _____
*(If spouse's income is to be considered,
spouse must submit Form I-864A.)*

Income of other qualifying persons.
*(List names; include spouse if applicable.
Each person must complete Form I-864A.)*

_____            $ _____

_____            $ _____

_____            $ _____

**Total Household Income**                 $ _____

Explain on separate sheet of paper if you or any of the above listed individuals were not required to file Federal income tax returns for the most recent 3 years, or if other explanation of income, employment, or evidence is necessary.

## E. Determination of Eligibility Based on Income

1. ☐ I am subject to the 125 percent of poverty line requirement for sponsors.
   ☐ I am subject to the 100 percent of poverty line requirement for sponsors on active duty in the U.S. Armed Forces sponsoring their spouse or child.
2. Sponsor's total household size, from Part 4.C., line 5 _____ .
3. Minimum income requirement from the Poverty Guidelines chart for the year _____ is $ _____
   for this household size.                                              *(year)*

**If you are currently employed and your household income for your household size is equal to or greater than the applicable poverty line requirement (from line E.3.), you do not need to list assets (Parts 4.F. and 5) or have a joint sponsor (Part 6)** unless you are requested to do so by a Consular or Immigration Officer. You may skip to Part 7, Use of the Affidavit of Support to Overcome Public Charge Ground of Admissibility. **Otherwise, you should continue with Part 4.F.**

## Part 4.   Eligibility to Sponsor      *(Continued)*

### F. Sponsor's Assets and Liabilities

Your assets and those of your qualifying household members and dependents may be used to demonstrate ability to maintain an income at or above 125 percent (or 100 percent, if applicable) of the poverty line *if* they are available for the support of the sponsored immigrant(s) and can readily be converted into cash within 1 year. The household member, other than the immigrant(s) you are sponsoring, must complete and sign Form I-864A, Contract Between Sponsor and Household Member. List the cash value of each asset *after* any debts or liens are subtracted. Supporting evidence must be attached to establish location, ownership, date of acquisition, and value of each asset listed, including any liens and liabilities related to each asset listed. See "Evidence of Assets" in Instructions.

| Type of Asset | Cash Value of Assets *(Subtract any debts)* |
|---|---|
| Savings deposits | $ |
| Stocks, bonds, certificates of deposit | $ |
| Life insurance cash value | $ |
| Real estate | $ |
| Other *(specify)* | $ |
| **Total Cash Value of Assets** | $            0.00 |

## Part 5.   Immigrant's Assets and Offsetting Liabilities

The sponsored immigrant's assets may also be used in support of your ability to maintain income at or above 125 percent of the poverty line *if* the assets are or will be available in the United States for the support of the sponsored immigrant(s) and can readily be converted into cash within 1 year.

The sponsored immigrant should provide information on his or her assets in a format similar to part 4.F. above. Supporting evidence must be attached to establish location, ownership, and value of each asset listed, including any liens and liabilities for each asset listed. See "Evidence of Assets" in Instructions.

## Part 6.   Joint Sponsors

If household income and assets do not meet the appropriate poverty line for your household size, a joint sponsor is required. There may be more than one joint sponsor, but each joint sponsor must individually meet the 125 percent of poverty line requirement based on his or her household income and/or assets, including any assets of the sponsored immigrant. By submitting a separate Affidavit of Support under Section 213A of the Act (Form I-864), a joint sponsor accepts joint responsibility with the petitioner for the sponsored immigrant(s) until they become U.S. citizens, can be credited with 40 quarters of work, leave the United States permanently, or die.

## Part 7.   Use of the Affidavit of Support to Overcome Public Charge Ground of Inadmissibility

Section 212(a)(4)(C) of the Immigration and Nationality Act provides that an alien seeking permanent residence as an immediate relative (including an orphan), as a family-sponsored immigrant, or as an alien who will accompany or follow to join another alien is considered to be likely to become a public charge and is inadmissible to the United States unless a sponsor submits a legally enforceable affidavit of support on behalf of the alien. Section 212(a)(4)(D) imposes the same requirement on an employment-based immigrant, and those aliens who accompany or follow to join the employment- based immigrant, if the employment-based immigrant will be employed by a relative, or by a firm in which a relative owns a significant interest. Separate affidavits of support are required for family members at the time they immigrate if they are not included on this affidavit of support or do not apply for an immigrant visa or adjustment of status within 6 months of the date this affidavit of support is originally signed. The sponsor must provide the sponsored immigrant(s) whatever support is necessary to maintain them at an income that is at least 125 percent of the Federal poverty guidelines.

> *I submit this affidavit of support in consideration of the sponsored immigrant(s) not being found inadmissible to the United States under section 212(a)(4)(C) (or 212(a)(4)(D) for an employment-based immigrant) and to enable the sponsored immigrant(s) to overcome this ground of inadmissibility. I agree to provide the sponsored immigrant(s) whatever support is necessary to maintain the sponsored immigrant(s) at an income that is at least 125 percent of the Federal poverty guidelines. I understand that my obligation will continue until my death or the sponsored immigrant(s) have become U.S. citizens, can be credited with 40 quarters of work, depart the United States permanently, or die.*

---

**Part 7.    Use of the Affidavit of Support to Overcome Public Charge Grounds**                    *(Continued)*

### Notice of Change of Address.

Sponsors are required to provide written notice of any change of address within 30 days of the change in address until the sponsored immigrant(s) have become U.S. citizens, can be credited with 40 quarters of work, depart the United States permanently, or die. To comply with this requirement, the sponsor must complete INS Form I-865. Failure to give this notice may subject the sponsor to the civil penalty established under section 213A(d)(2) which ranges from $250 to $2,000, unless the failure to report occurred with the knowledge that the sponsored immigrant(s) had received means-tested public benefits, in which case the penalty ranges from $2,000 to $5,000.

> *If my address changes for any reason before my obligations under this affidavit of support terminate, I will complete and file INS Form I-865, Sponsor's Notice of Change of Address, within 30 days of the change of address. I understand that failure to give this notice may subject me to civil penalties.*

### Means-tested Public Benefit Prohibitions and Exceptions.

Under section 403(a) of Public Law 104-193 (Welfare Reform Act), aliens lawfully admitted for permanent residence in the United States, with certain exceptions, are ineligible for most Federally-funded means-tested public benefits during their first 5 years in the United States. This provision does not apply to public benefits specified in section 403(c) of the Welfare Reform Act or to State public benefits, including emergency Medicaid; short-term, non-cash emergency relief; services provided under the National School Lunch and Child Nutrition Acts; immunizations and testing and treatment for communicable diseases; student assistance under the Higher Education Act and the Public Health Service Act; certain forms of foster-care or adoption assistance under the Social Security Act; Head Start programs; means-tested programs under the Elementary and Secondary Education Act; and Job Training Partnership Act programs.

### Consideration of Sponsor's Income in Determining Eligibility for Benefits.

If a permanent resident alien is no longer statutorily barred from a Federally-funded means-tested public benefit program and applies for such a benefit, the income and resources of the sponsor and the sponsor's spouse will be considered (or deemed) to be the income and resources of the sponsored immigrant in determining the immigrant's eligibility for Federal means-tested public benefits. Any State or local government may also choose to consider (or deem) the income and resources of the sponsor and the sponsor's spouse to be the income and resources of the immigrant for the purposes of determining eligibility for their means-tested public benefits. The attribution of the income and resources of the sponsor and the sponsor's spouse to the immigrant will continue until the immigrant becomes a U.S. citizen or has worked or can be credited with 40 qualifying quarters of work, provided that the immigrant or the worker crediting the quarters to the immigrant has not received any Federal means-tested public benefit during any creditable quarter for any period after December 31, 1996.

> *I understand that, under section 213A of the Immigration and Nationality Act (the Act), as amended, this affidavit of support constitutes a contract between me and the U.S. Government. This contract is designed to protect the United States Government, and State and local government agencies or private entities that provide means-tested public benefits, from having to pay benefits to or on behalf of the sponsored immigrant(s), for as long as I am obligated to support them under this affidavit of support. I understand that the sponsored immigrants, or any Federal, State, local, or private entity that pays any means-tested benefit to or on behalf of the sponsored immigrant(s), are entitled to sue me if I fail to meet my obligations under this affidavit of support, as defined by section 213A and INS regulations.*

### Civil Action to Enforce.

If the immigrant on whose behalf this affidavit of support is executed receives any Federal, State, or local means-tested public benefit before this obligation terminates, the Federal, State, or local agency or private entity may request reimbursement from the sponsor who signed this affidavit. If the sponsor fails to honor the request for reimbursement, the agency may sue the sponsor in any U.S. District Court or any State court with jurisdiction of civil actions for breach of contract. INS will provide names, addresses, and Social Security account numbers of sponsors to benefit-providing agencies for this purpose. Sponsors may also be liable for paying the costs of collection, including legal fees.

---

---

**Part 7.** Use of the Affidavit of Support to Overcome Public Charge Grounds *(Continued)*

---

*I acknowledge that section 213A(a)(1)(B) of the Act grants the sponsored immigrant(s) and any Federal, State, local, or private agency that pays any means-tested public benefit to or on behalf of the sponsored immigrant(s) standing to sue me for failing to meet my obligations under this affidavit of support. I agree to submit to the personal jurisdiction of any court of the United States or of any State, territory, or possession of the United States if the court has subject matter jurisdiction of a civil lawsuit to enforce this affidavit of support. I agree that no lawsuit to enforce this affidavit of support shall be barred by any statute of limitations that might otherwise apply, so long as the plaintiff initiates the civil lawsuit no later than ten (10) years after the date on which a sponsored immigrant last received any means-tested public benefits.*

## Collection of Judgment.

*I acknowledge that a plaintiff may seek specific performance of my support obligation. Furthermore, any money judgment against me based on this affidavit of support may be collected through the use of a judgment lien under 28 U.S.C 3201, a writ of execution under 28 U.S.C 3203, a judicial installment payment order under 28 U.S.C 3204, garnishment under 28 U.S.C 3205, or through the use of any corresponding remedy under State law. I may also be held liable for costs of collection, including attorney fees.*

## Concluding Provisions.

I, _____ , *certify under penalty of perjury under the laws of the United*

States that:

    *(a) I know the contents of this affidavit of support signed by me;*

    *(b) All the statements in this affidavit of support are true and correct,*

    *(c) I make this affidavit of support for the consideration stated in Part 7, freely, and*
        *without any mental reservation or purpose of evasion;*

    *(d) Income tax returns submitted in support of this affidavit are true copies of the returns*
        *filed with the Internal Revenue Service; and*

    *(e) Any other evidence submitted is true and correct.*

---

          *(Sponsor's Signature)*                  *(Date)*

Subscribed and sworn to (or affirmed) before me this

_____ day of _____ , _____
               *(Month)*       *(Year)*

at   _____ .

My commission expires on  _____ .

---

*(Signature of Notary Public or Officer Administering Oath)*

---

          *(Title)*

---

**Part 8.** If someone other than the sponsor prepared this affidavit of support, that person must complete the following:

---

I certify under penalty of perjury under the laws of the United States that I prepared this affidavit of support at the sponsor's request, and that this affidavit of support is based on all information of which I have knowledge.

| Signature | Print Your Name | Date | Daytime Telephone Number |
|---|---|---|---|
| | | | |

Firm Name and Address

# CONSUMER BROCHURES FROM NCLC

## *Order Form*

**Consumer Education Brochures** *(Intended to be distributed directly to older consumers).* *NO CHARGE FOR FIRST 20. CHARGE FOR BULK ORDERS IS $40 FOR EACH ADDITIONAL 100 BROCHURES. MAXIMUM ORDER IS 200*

_____ What You Should Know About Debt Collection

Shopping for Money Wire Services: Five Steps You Can Take to Avoid Fraud and Save Money

| _____ENGLISH | _____SPANISH | _____CHINESE | _____RUSSIAN |
| _____KOREAN | _____VIETNAMESE | | |

Stop Phone Slamming

| _____ENGLISH | _____SPANISH | _____CHINESE | _____RUSSIAN |
| _____KOREAN | _____VIETNAMESE | | |

Borrower Beware: The High Cost of Small Loans, Pawn Brokers and Rent-to-Own Stores

| _____ENGLISH | _____SPANISH | _____VIETNAMESE | _____RUSSIAN |
| _____KOREAN | _____CHINESE | | |

Cashing Checks and Opening Bank Accounts: How to Save Money and Avoid Theft

| _____ENGLISH | _____SPANISH | _____VIETNAMESE | _____RUSSIAN |
| _____KOREAN | _____CHINESE | | |

The Truth About Credit Reports and Credit Repair Companies

_____ENGLISH  _____SPANISH  _____VIETNAMESE  _____RUSSIAN

_____KOREAN  _____CHINESE

_____ Your Legal Rights During and After Bankruptcy

_____ Using Credit Wisely After Bankruptcy

## Consumer Concerns for IMMIGRANTS (*These newsletters are designed to help advocates and service providers spot consumer problems and determine when clients should be referred for legal assistance*). *NO CHARGE – MAXIMUM ORDER IS 10 OF EACH*

_____ High Cost of Financial Services, Loans, and Rent-to-Own for Low-Income Borrowers: The Challenges of the Private Marketplace

## Consumer Facts for IMMIGRANTS (*Intended to be distributed directly to immigrant consumers*). *NO CHARGE – MAXIMUM ORDER IS 10 OF EACH*

_____ Beware of Dishonest Immigration Consultants

## Consumer Concerns for OLDER AMERICANS (*These newsletters are designed to help advocates and service providers spot consumer problems and determine when clients should be referred for legal assistance*). *NO CHARGE – MAXIMUM ORDER IS 10 OF EACH*

_____ Advice for Seniors About Credit Cards

_____ Avoiding Living Trust Scams: A Quick Guide For Advocates

_____ Dealing with Utility Companies Regarding Disputed Bills and Utility Deposits

_____ Electronic Funds Transfer: What Senior Advocates Should Know About Electronic Deposit of Social Security and SSI

_____ Helping Elderly Homeowners Victimized By Predatory Scams Mortgage Loans

_____ Home Improvement Scams Alert

_____ How to Help Older Americans Avoid Loss of Utility Services

_____ INTERNET RESOURCES: Helpful Consumer and Elder Law Web Sites

_____ Medical Debt and Seniors: How Consumer Law Can Help

_____ Spending the House: A Quick Guide for Advocates on Reverse Mortgages

_____ Steps That Advocates Can Take to Help Prevent Foreclosure
_____ What To Do When Utility Service Has Been Disconnected

_____ When You Can't Go Home Again: Using Consumer Law to Protect Nursing Facility Residents

## Consumer Facts for OLDER AMERICANS *(Intended to be distributed directly to older consumers).* NO CHARGE – MAXIMUM ORDER OF 10 OF EACH

_____ Protect Your Investment - Don't Let Predatory Lenders Take Your Home!

_____ Tips For Seniors On Living Trusts

_____ Tips For Consumers On Reverse Mortgages

_____ What To Do If You've Become The Victim of Telemarketing Fraud

_____ What You Should Know About Refinancing

_____ When Your Social Security Benefits Are Taken To Pay Back Money To The Federal Government

## Other Brochures for ELDER LAW ADVOCATES. NO CHARGE – MAXIMUM ORDER IS 25 OF EACH

_____ CONSUMER LAW... Why is it Relevant to the Legal Defense of Older Americans?

_____ Overview of Services: National Legal Resource Initiative for Financially Distressed Older Americans

## Bulk orders must be pre-paid and are subject to availability. Prices include shipping and handling. To place an order mail or fax this completed order form to the attention of Debbie Parziale at 617/523-7398. Enclosed is an order form and check in the amount of $_____ payable to the National Consumer Law Center, 77 Summer Street, 10th Floor, Boston, MA 02110-1006. Please send the quantity of brochures indicated above to:

Name_____

Organization_____

Address_____

City_____ State _____ Zip_____

Phone _____ Fax _____

Email _____

**Please Charge Credit Card:**
VISA/MasterCard _____-_____-_____-_____

Expiration Date _____/_____/_____

Signature _____

*National Consumer Law Center, Inc. – 77 Summer Street, 10th Floor*
*Boston, MA 02110-1006*
*Phone: 617/523-8010; Fax: 617/523-7398; Email:*          ;
*Web: www.consumerlaw.org*

## -- Appendix 4 --

# NCLC PUBLICATIONS

**The Consumer Credit and Sales Legal Practice Series** contains 16 titles, each with a CD-Rom that allows users to copy information directly onto a word processor. Each manual is designed to be an attorney's primary practice guide and legal resource when representing clients in all fifty states on that consumer law topic, and is updated annually. The 16 titles are arranged into four "libraries," and are available individually or as a set.

### *DEBTOR RIGHTS LIBRARY*

**Consumer Bankruptcy Law and Practice**: (6th ed. and Supp. and CD-Rom) the definitive personal bankruptcy manual with step-by-step instructions from initial interview to final discharge and including consumers' rights as creditors when a merchant or landlord files for bankruptcy. Appendices and CD-Rom contain over 130 annotated pleadings, bankruptcy statutes, rules and fee schedules, an interview questionnaire, a client handout, and software to complete petitions and schedules.

**Fair Debt Collection** (4th ed. and Supp. and CD-Rom): the basic reference in the field, covering the Fair Debt Collection Practices Act and common law, state statutory and other federal debt collection protections. Appendices and companion CD-Rom contain numerous practice aids, including sample pleadings and discovery materials, the FDCPA, the FTC's Official Staff Commentary, <u>all</u> FTC staff opinion letters, and summaries of reported and unreported cases.

**Repossessions and Foreclosures** (4ᵗʰ ed. and Supp. and CD-Rom): unique guide to home foreclosures, car and mobile home repossessions, threatened seizures of household goods, tax and other statutory liens, and default remedies relating to automobile leases and rent-to-own transactions. Appendices and CD-Rom reprint relevant UCC provisions and comments, summarize all state foreclosure and right-to-cure laws, and present various sample pleadings.

**Student Loan Law** (with CD-Rom): student loan debt collection and collection fees; discharges based on closed school, false certification, failure to refund, disability, and bankruptcy; tax intercepts, wage garnishment, and offset of social security benefits; repayment plans, consolidation loans, and deferments, and non-payment of loan based on school fraud. CD-Rom and appendices contain numerous forms, pleadings, interpretation letters and regulations.

**Access to Utility Service** (2d ed. and CD-Rom): the only examination of consumer rights when dealing with regulated, de-regulated, and unregulated utilities, covering electric, gas, oil, propane, and other fuels, and telecommunications. Everything from terminations and billing errors to low-income payment plans, fuel allowances in subsidized housing, LIHEAP, and weatherization. Includes summaries of state utility regulations, key statutes and regulations.

## *CREDIT AND BANKING LIBRARY*

**Truth in Lending** (4ᵗʰ ed. and Supp. and CD-Rom): detailed analysis of all aspects of TILA, the Consumer Leasing Act, and the Home Ownership and Equity Protection Act. Appendices and the CD-Rom contain the Acts, Reg. Z, Reg. M, and their Official Staff Commentaries, sample pleadings and rescission notice, and a program to compute APRs.

**Fair Credit Reporting Act** (4ᵗʰ ed. and Supp. and CD-Rom): the key resource for handling any type of credit reporting issue, from cleaning up blemished credit records to obtaining credit despite negative information to suing reporting agencies and creditors for inaccurate reports. Covers the FCRA, the Credit Repair Organizations Act, state credit reporting and repair statutes and common law claims.

**Consumer Banking and Payments Law** (with CD-Rom): unique analysis of consumer law as to checks, money orders, and international wires; credit, debit, ATM, and stored value cards; banker's right of set off; electronic transfer of food stamps and other state benefits, direct deposits of federal payments, and other electronic transfers. The CD-Rom and appendices reprint relevant statutes, regulations, and interpretations.

**The Cost of Credit: Regulation and Legal Challenges** (2d ed. and Supp. and CD-Rom): a one-of-a-kind resource detailing state and federal regulation of consumer credit in all fifty states, federal usury preemption, explaining credit math, and how to challenge excessive credit charges and credit insurance. The CD-Rom includes a credit math program and hard-to-find agency interpretations.

**Credit Discrimination** (2d. ed. and Supp. and CD-Rom): analysis of the Equal Credit Opportunity Act, Fair Housing Act, Civil Rights Acts, and state statutes concerning discrimination in mortgages and other credit transactions, including reprints of federal statutes, FRB Reg. B and Commentary, HUD fair housing regulations, sample pleadings, and consent agreements.

## *CONSUMER LITIGATION LIBRARY*

**Consumer Arbitration Agreements** (with CD-Rom): numerous approaches to challenge the enforceability of a binding arbitration agreement, the interrelation of the Federal Arbitration Act and state law, class actions in arbitration, the right to discovery, and other topics. Appendices and CD-Rom include sample discovery, numerous briefs, and the rules of the two major arbitration mechanisms.

**Consumer Class Actions: A Practical Litigation Guide** (4th ed. and CD-Rom): makes class action litigation manageable even for small offices, including numerous sample pleadings, class certification memoranda, discovery, class notices and settlement materials.

**Consumer Law Pleadings on CD-Rom** (Cumulative CD-Rom and Index Guide to *all* pleadings from *all* NCLC manuals): Over 600 notable recent pleadings from all types of consumer cases--home foreclosures, landlord-tenant, mobile homes, car cases, debt collection, fair credit reporting, home improvement fraud, flipping, yield spread premiums, fringe lending, rent to own, student loans, mandatory arbitration clauses, force-placed insurance, lender liability, and many others. Special finding aids pinpoint the desired pleading in seconds, ready to paste into a word processing program.

## DECEPTION AND WARRANTIES LIBRARY

**Unfair and Deceptive Acts and Practices** (5th ed. and CD-Rom): the only practice manual covering all aspects of a deceptive practices case in every state. Special sections on automobile sales, the federal racketeering (RICO) statute, unfair insurance practices, and the FTC Holder Rule.

**Automobile Fraud** (with Supp. and CD-Rom)**:** detailed examination of odometer tampering, lemon laundering, sale of salvage, wrecked, and flood-damaged cars, undisclosed damage to new cars, and deception as to prior use, litigating fraud claims for punitive damages, numerous sample pleadings, and investigating a car's prior history, including state procedures for title searches.

**Consumer Warranty Law** (2d ed. and CD-Rom): comprehensive treatment of state new and used car lemon laws, the federal Magnuson-Moss Warranty Act, UCC Articles 2 and 2A, mobile home warranty legislation, new home warranty law, FTC Used Car Rule, negligence and strict liability theories, car repair and home improvement statutes, service contract and lease laws. Also includes sample pleadings and discovery, notice of revocation, and other practice aids.

# OTHER NCLC PUBLICATIONS

**Consumer Law in a Box**: a CD-Rom combining all documents and software from 16 other NCLC CD-Roms. Allows one to quickly pinpoint the correct document from thousands found on the CD through key word searches and Internet-style navigation, links, bookmarks, and other finding aids. Includes two credit math programs and bankruptcy software.

**NCLC REPORTS** newsletter covers the latest developments and ideas in the practice of consumer law, and is issued 24 times a year.

**STOP Predatory Lending: A Guide for Legal Advocates** (with CD-Rom due out in early 2002): provides a roadmap and practical legal strategy and resources on litigating the range of predatory lending abuse from small loans to abusive mortgage loans. The CD-Rom contains a credit math program, pleadings, legislative and administrative materials, and underwriting guidelines.

**Sourcebook of the Annual National Consumer Rights Litigation Conference (with Disk)**: once a year, the nation's top consumer law practitioners share what works for them, with practical advice, sample pleadings, new legal developments, novel theories, and key cases.

**Surviving Debt: A Guide for Consumers** (3$^{rd}$ ed.): A great overview of consumer law. Everything a paralegal, new attorney, or client needs to know about debt collectors, managing credit card debt, whether to refinance, credit card problems, home foreclosures, evictions, repossessions, credit reporting, utility terminations, student loans, budgeting, and bankruptcy.

**NCLC Guide to How to Buy a Manufactured Home:** what consumers and their advocates need to know about mobile home dealer sales practices and what to look for in-depth about mobile home quality and defects, with numerous photographs and construction details.

**Return to Sender: Getting a Refund or Replacement for Your Lemon Car:** Find how lemon laws work, what consumers and their lawyers should know to evaluate each other, investigative techniques and discovery tips, how to handle both informal dispute resolution and trials, and more.

# *To Order*

To order **The NCLC Guide on Consumer Rights for Immigrants**, contact your local bookstore, or order directly from National Consumer Law Center by sending $10 (shipping and handling included) for each copy. Discounts are available for bulk orders. Please call (617) 523-8089 for MasterCard/Visa orders and for bulk discount orders. Send your check to:

Send your check to:
**National Consumer Law Center**
**77 Summer Street, 10<sup>th</sup> Floor**
**Boston, MA 02110**

**(617) 523-8089**
**Fax  (617) 523-7398**
**email: publications@nclc.org**

(Qualified legal services, and nonprofit agencies assisting immigrants can receive complimentary copies. Contact NCLC by FAX at (617) 523-7398 or the address above for these requests.)

**Visit National Consumer Law Center on the web:**

**www.consumerlaw.org**